Some of the Descendants of Thomas and Sarah Webster

of England and New Hampshire

Dale Douglas Webster

HERITAGE BOOKS
2009

HERITAGE BOOKS
AN IMPRINT OF HERITAGE BOOKS, INC.

Books, CDs, and more—Worldwide

For our listing of thousands of titles see our website
at
www.HeritageBooks.com

Published 2009 by
HERITAGE BOOKS, INC.
Publishing Division
100 Railroad Ave. #104
Westminster, Maryland 21157

Copyright © 2009 Dale Douglas Webster

Other books by the author:
The Descendants of Dutch Mennonites, Peter and Anna Berg of the Ukraine and Kansas
The Descendants of Jacob and Mary Moomey of Pennsylvania, Maryland, Ohio and Iowa
The Descendants of James and Deborah Oldfield of Indiana, Iowa and Kansas
The Descendants of Johan Frederick Solter of Germany, Illinois and Kansas
The Descendants of Samuel and Deborah Webster of Vermont, New York and Ohio

All rights reserved. No part of this book may be reproduced or transmitted in any form or by any means, electronic or mechanical, including photocopying, recording or by any information storage and retrieval system without written permission from the author, except for the inclusion of brief quotations in a review.

International Standard Book Numbers
Paperbound: 978-0-7884-4927-7
Clothbound: 978-0-7884-8178-9

Dedication

This work is dedicated to the memory of the late Howard Emerson Webster of Iowa who started this family history research. It was his passion. He and his devoted wife, Bernice, gathered the information that is the foundation for this genealogy.

TABLE OF CONTENTS

Table of Illustrations ………………………… vii

Reading This Book ………………………… ix

Acknowledgments …………………………….. xi

Introduction ………………………………… xiii

First Generation………………………….. .. 1

Second Generation……………………….. 5

Third Generation………………………… 11

Fourth Generation………..………………. 19

Fifth Generation…………………………. 31

Sixth Generation………………………… 63

Seventh Generation………..……………… 81

Eighth Generation………………………… 99

Ninth Generation………………………… 111

Tenth Generation………………………… 129

Eleventh Generation……………………… 151

Twelfth Generation.. 163

Index of Names.. 165

About the Author 183

TABLE OF ILLUSTRATIONS

Figure 1 - Map of Vermont and New Hampshire   2

Figure 2 - Map of New York   37

Figure 3 – Map of Ohio   38

Figure 4 – Map of Iowa   66

Figure 5 – John and Mary Webster   68

Figure 6 – John Webster's Brick Factory.........   70

Figure 7 – Children of John and Mary Webster   71

Figure 8 – Lyman Green and Nancy O. Webster   79

Figure 9 – Map of Kansas   90

Figure 10 – William Daniel and Nancy Jane ..   93
Webster and their children

Figure 11 - Frehling and Florence Webster and   97
their children

Figure 12 – Reginald and Julia Webster.............   120

Figure 13 – Shirley Knight   139

Reading This Book

If, while reading the following pages of this book, the reader will keep these few facts in mind, a much clearer understanding of the contents will result. The format or style used in this book is known as the **Modified Register System,** which has been refined by the National Genealogical Society.

Three types of numbers are used: one to uniquely identify the individual, one to indicate the generation into which that person falls, and one to denote his or her birth-order within the nuclear family. The identification numbering system used in this book is called **By Generation**. The starting person is 1, his first child is 2. All the children are listed as generation number two, the grandchildren are listed as generation number three and so on. Each person is assigned an ID number in sequential order by generation.

When an individual is introduced in his/her separate sketch, the name appears in boldface letters. The identification number precedes the name. The last given name is followed immediately by a superscript number indicating the number of generations from the starting individual in this book. In parentheses following the name is a list of direct ancestors back to the starting individual. Only the given name is listed, preceded by his/her ID number, and followed by the generation number in superscript.

When the list of children is presented, the plus (+) sign indicates that more about this child will be presented in his/her separate sketch. The ID number is printed. Next, a small roman numeral in front of the name designates birth-order. Next, the name is followed by the birth and death dates.

The term "Spouse" may have several different meanings: husband, wife, partner, mate, or significant other. The couple involved may not be legally married. The term "stepchild" may have several different meanings: the child may be a stepchild, adopted child, foster child, or just raised in the home. If there are any other children of the spouse, they will be designated as stepchildren.

The index is arranged alphabetically by surname. Under each surname, the given names are alphabetically arranged. The name is followed by the year of birth and death in square brackets. The number to the right indicates the page where this name appears. The wife appears under her maiden name and under her married names with her maiden name in parentheses.

Acknowledgments

This genealogy of some of the descendents of Thomas and Sarah Webster is based on research by Webster family members and three professional genealogists.

Prominent among the family member researchers was the late Howard E. Webster of Iowa. His efforts with the assistance of his wife, Bernice, started this work and deserve much of the credit. Also, I have special thanks to my Aunt Elaine (Webster) Wilson for much valuable family information and to my wife, Kathleen, for editorial assistance and encouragement.

The three contributing professional genealogists were: Alice Eichholz of Vermont, Ph.D. and Certified Genealogist; Alicia Williams of Massachusetts, editor of *The Mayflower Descendant* journal; and Melinde Lutz Sanborn of New Hampshire, a well known specialist in forensic and historical genealogical research. Their discoveries extended the work from frontier to colonial times and told us the backgrounds of Thomas and Sarah Webster.

The author compiled this genealogy mostly from primary source documents, such as birth and death certificates and census records. Very little, except for the oldest and the most recent information, came from family or secondary sources. The information presented here is based on a solid foundation of support material, except in two places where it will be pointed out why the facts lead to the support for claims of lineage.

Introduction

By way of overview, this history extends back to the 1500s and covers some of the earliest colonial settlements of the New World. A total of 452 descendants are identified in twelve generations. Additionally, there are presented five Mayflower Pilgrim lines including the most famous ones, such as Miles Standish and John Alden. Also, included in this line is the famous Senator and Secretary of State, Daniel Webster. There are several Revolutionary and Civil War soldiers and pioneers who first settled the frontiers of the United States.

Most of our ancestors were British, and they represent a combination of many influences throughout the last two thousand years. The British Isles have been invaded and conquered by many people, and their cultures mixed to produce British civilization. We will set the context here for the family history to come in the following chapters.

The early inhabitants of the British Isles were the Gaels as they called themselves, or the Celts as the Romans called them. From 43 to 79 A.D., the Romans conquered southern Britain and occupied it until the fall of Rome in 476 A.D.[1] They were never able to conquer three Gaelic tribes: the Picts, the Scots and, the Irish; but the other Gaelic people were subdued and adopted many Roman customs, the

---

[1] McEvedy, Colin, *The Penguin Atlas of Ancient History*, Penguin Books, 1967, New York, pages 79-92.

Introduction

language, government structure, art, and technology. In addition, the Romans spread their adopted Catholic Christian religion to even the Irish. Saint Patrick who is given credit to converting the Irish was in fact a Roman.

Before Rome fell, it was coming under increased pressure from barbarian hordes, and the Romans abandoned Britain around 411 A.D. to consolidate their positions at the European frontiers.[2] The defensive void and the Celtic anarchy that resulted allowed three Teutonic tribes, the Angles, the Saxons, and Jutes, to raid and settle the eastern parts of Britain over the next three hundred years. The legendary Celtic King Arthur tried to stop this invasion but was unsuccessful, and the Breton Gaelic people were driven north to Scotland, west to Wales, Cornwall, and Ireland, and south across the Channel to Brittany giving that French peninsula its name. The Anglo-Saxon settlement of eastern Britain became so strong that it became known as Englaland, meaning land of the Angles, from which the name England was derived.

More Teutonic raiders, invaders, and settlers came from Norway and Denmark with the Viking Age from 700 to 1000 A.D. The Norse and Danes settled generally on the coasts of the British Isles, founded Dublin, Ireland, and ruled northeast England around York, or Jorvik as they called it. In 1066 A.D., a descendant of Vikings who settled in Normandy, France, disputed the throne of

---

[2] McEvedy, Colin, *The Penguin Atlas of Medieval History*, Penguin Books, 1961, New York, page 18.

Introduction

England with his Viking cousins and won the Battle of Hastings to take the crown. William "the Conqueror," the Duke of Normandy, ruled England as king and brought the French language and culture to Britain. French became the royal court language and merged with Germanic Old English to make modern English. So the Gaelic, Roman, and Teutonic cultures combined to make the British culture we know.

Another very important era that directly affected our ancestors was the Reformation of the Church. Religion dominated life in the Middle Ages, and Catholicism was accepted by all the people in the British Isles, even though some vestiges of their old religions persisted. However, the Church was corrupt and oppressive to a great degree. The Church hierarchy, especially at the Bishop level, had powers to tax and jail people and used them in tyrannical ways. They profited immensely from their elaborate fee and fine system known as Indulgences.[3] This system in particular incensed some members of the clergy, such as Martin Luther, to protest in 1517 and start the Protestant Movement. This effort to reform the Church caused much chaos throughout Europe for the next few hundred years.

King Henry VIII seized the Reformation Movement as a reason to break away from the Roman Catholic Church and set himself up as the head of the Church of England, also called the Anglican Church in 1532.[4] This action cut off the

---

[3] Willison, George F., *Saints and Strangers*, Parnassus Imprints, Inc., 1945, Orleans, Massachusetts, page 27.

[4] Grun, Bernard, *The Time Tables of History*, Simon and Schuster,

Introduction

flow of British Church money to Rome and redirected it to the Royal Treasury. It also permitted him to divorce his wife in order to find a woman who could give him a male heir. However, Henry did not change the Church hierarchy and the services very much. Many people were dissatisfied with the changes or lack of changes.

Several dissident factions formed. Most people accepted the Church of England, some left England to stay loyal to the Catholic Church, and many wanted changes that were being developed by Protestants in Europe allowing wider latitude in conducting services. Of the later, there were two main schools of thought. The first were those who wanted a purer and stricter interpretation of the Scriptures and believed they could change the Church of England from within. This group became known as the Puritans. The second were those who also wanted stricter interpretation of the Scriptures but did not like the hierarchy and wanted to separate from the Church of England. These people were known as Separatists and were considered renegades and religious fugitives in many cases.

The Mayflower Pilgrims were Separatists who first immigrated to Holland and then to the New World to found Plymouth Colony. The Puritans, a much larger faction, tried to change the Church of England, eventually fought the English Civil War over these issues, and won it in 1646.[5] This civil strife caused many Puritans to immigrate

---

1963, New York, page 236.

[5] Atmore, Anthony et al, *The Last Two Million Years*, The Reader's Digest Association, 1973, London, page 459.

Introduction

to the New World where they founded the Massachusetts Colony.

Our Webster ancestors, whose stories will be told in the following chapters, were among these groups and were motivated by these religious forces to come to the New World.

The surname of Webster is of Teutonic origin and is a combination of web and spinster meaning the occupation of female weaver but in Middle English it was also used by men. The name was taken by Flemish master weavers who came to England before 1200 A.D. to work in the thriving British wool industry. This is the period when people started using surnames. It originated in England's Yorkshire area, the center of the wool industry, which was settled mainly by Norse and Danish Vikings. It is also found in nearby Scotland where Webster belongs to the MacFarlane clan. There are several variations of spelling: Webstere, Webester, Webbster, Webstar, and Webster, which is the one in most common use.[6]

Records indicate that Webster families in early England were mostly of the landed gentry and yeoman classes in the Midlands. The earliest records of the name of Webster in England, are of John le Webestere of Norfolk County in the year 1273 and Robertus and Wilhelmus Webester of Yorkshire in 1379. The most important English family of

---

[6] Cottle, R., *Penguin Dictionary of Surnames*, Penguin Books, 1960, New York, pages 307 and 308.

Introduction

the name was that of John Webster of Derbyshire, whom King Henry IV granted large estates in 1400. There was also a John Webster (1580-1625) who was a noted playwright in London whose tragedies were ranked second only to William Shakespeare.[7]

Although we probably go back to common ancestors, there are three main lines of Webster families in the United States. One originates from John Webster of Ipswich, Massachusetts. We are not from this group. A second line is that from John Webster, the fifth Colonial Governor of Connecticut. We did not know this at the start of this research but my wife, Kathleen, is from this line. We say we are kissing cousins. Noah Webster, who wrote the first English dictionary and standardized spelling and pronunciation, is in this line. The third Webster line is ours and will be discussed in the first chapter. It is from Thomas Webster of Ormesby, Norfolk County, England that we descend.

Our ancestral home of Norfolk County, England is in East Anglia and is bounded to the north and east by the North

---

[7] Webster, Walter N., *An Historical Sketch of the Ancestry and Descendants of Henry Kingman Webster*, Self Published, 1985, Lawrence, Massachusetts, pages iii and iv..

Introduction

Sea. It is a low-lying area with heaths and salt marshes. On the east coast where Ormesby is located, there is a network of miles of lagoons connected by streams. There are windmills and dikes there like Holland.[8] Ormesby is now known as Ormesby Saint Margaret and is about 25 miles east-northeast of the city of Norwich.

---

[8] Porter, Darwin, *FROMMER'S Comprehensive Travel Guide: England & Scotland Ô91*, Prentis Hall Press, 1991, New York, page 456.

First Generation

1. **Thomas**[1] **Webster**, born 20 Nov 1631 in Ormesby, Norfolk Co., England; died 5 Jan 1715 in Hampton, Rockingham Co., New Hampshire, son of Thomas Webster and Margaret (Margery) (---).[9] He married on 2 Nov 1657 in Hampton, Rockingham Co., New Hampshire **Sarah Brewer**, born 1636 in Hampton, Rockingham Co., New Hampshire; died 15 Feb 1717 in Hampton, Rockingham Co., New Hampshire, daughter of Thomas Brewer and Elizabeth Graves.

Thomas's father died at Ormesby, Norfolk County, England, on 30 April 1634. Thomas was only two and a half years old at the time. His mother remarried. About two years later in 1636, Thomas was brought to America by his mother, Margery, and his stepfather, Deacon William Godfrey. They first landed in Watertown, Massachusetts, and shortly moved to Hampton, Rockingham County, New Hampshire. Hampton is about 15 miles south southwest of Portsmouth. Thomas and Sarah lived in Hampton on Drake Road near Webster's Brook.

Thomas fought in the Indian Wars in 1675. He also served as a Grand Juror at Portsmouth in 1682 and as a collector of taxes in Hampton in 1693. We are not sure about his other vocations, but service as a juror and a tax collector shows that he must have been literate.

---

[9] Webster, Prentiss, "One Branch of the Webster Family from Thomas Webster of Ormesby, County Norfolk, England," 1894, Lowell Courier Publishing Company, Lowell, Mass, p. 10.

First Generation

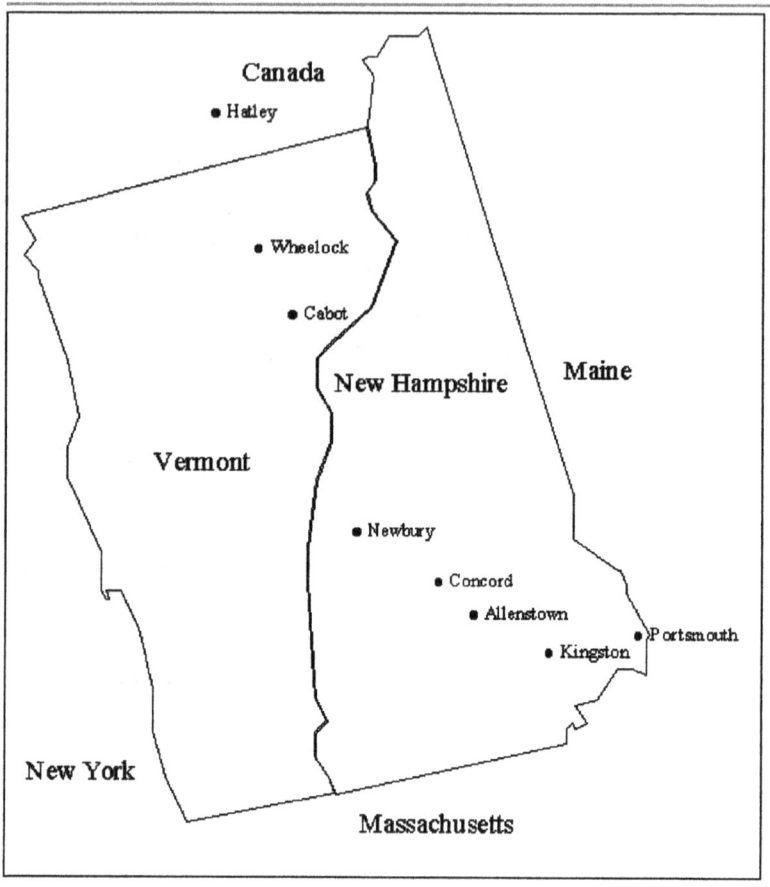

Figure 1 – Map of Vermont and New Hampshire showing relevant points.

Thomas[1] and Sarah (Brewer) Webster are the common ancestors of two notable third cousins four generations away. One cousin is Samuel[5] Webster (1778-1847) of our direct line, and the other cousin is the famous Honorable

First Generation

Daniel Webster (1782-1852), the great orator, U.S. Senator, and Secretary of State under three presidents. Daniel springs from Thomas^1's and Sarah's son, Ebenezer, and our Samuel^6 comes from their son, Thomas^2, Jr.:

Children of Thomas Webster and Sarah Brewer were as follows:

+ 2   i   **Mary^2 Webster**, born 10 Aug 1657 in Hampton, Rockingham Co., New Hampshire; died after 1735 in Hampton, Rockingham Co., New Hampshire. She married (1) **William Swaine**; (2) **Joseph Emmons**.

+ 3   ii   **Sarah^2 Webster**, born 21 Jan 1660 in Hampton, Rockingham Co., New Hampshire; died 5 Jan 1745 in Hampton, Rockingham Co., New Hampshire. She married **William Lane**.

   4   iii   **Hannah^2 Webster**, born 27 Dec 1663 in Hampton, Rockingham Co., New Hampshire; died 1 Feb 1664 in Hampton, Rockingham Co., New Hampshire.

+ 5   iv   **Thomas^2 Webster Jr.**, born 20 Nov 1664 in Hampton, Rockingham Co., New Hampshire; died 7 Mar 1733 in Kingston, Rockingham Co., New Hampshire. He married **Sarah Godfrey**.

+ 6   v   **Ebenezer^2 Webster**, born 1 Aug 1667 in Hampton, Rockingham Co., New Hampshire; died 21 Feb 1756 in Kingston, Rockingham Co., New Hampshire. He

First Generation

		married **Hannah Judkins**.
7	vi	**Isaac² Webster**, born 20 Apr 1670 in Hampton, Rockingham Co., New Hampshire; died 21 Feb 1718 in Kingston, Rockingham Co., New Hampshire. He married on 2 Apr 1697 **Mary Hutchins**.
8	vii	**John² Webster**, born 16 Feb 1674 in Hampton, Rockingham Co., New Hampshire; died after 1752 in Hampton Falls, Rockingham Co., New Hampshire. He married (1) on 21 Sep 1703 **Abiah Shaw**; (2) **Sarah (---)**.
9	viii	**Joshua² Webster** , born 20 Jun 1676 in Hampton, Rockingham Co., New Hampshire; died 25 Oct 1725.
+ 10	ix	**Abigail² Webster**, born 1 Jan 1679 in Hampton, Rockingham Co., New Hampshire; died 3 Aug 1758 in Hampton, Rockingham Co., New Hampshire. She married **John Nay**.

Second Generation

The children of Thomas and Sarah Webster lived entirely during the colonial period of the history of the United States of America. They were mostly devout Puritans and loyal subjects to the British Crown. They lived in settlements very close to the ocean shore and established a foothold in a difficult wilderness.

2. **Mary**^{2} **Webster** (Thomas^1), born 10 Aug 1657 in Hampton, Rockingham Co., New Hampshire; died after 1735 in Hampton, Rockingham Co., New Hampshire. She married (1) on 20 Oct 1676 in Hampton, Rockingham Co., New Hampshire **William Swaine**, born <1654> in Hampton, Rockingham Co., New Hampshire; died after 9 Apr 1692 in Hampton, Rockingham Co., New Hampshire, son of William Swaine and Prudence Marston; (2) on 12 Jun 1694 **Joseph Emmons**, born 1654 in Hampton, Rockingham Co., New Hampshire.

Children of Mary Webster and William Swaine were as follows:

11	i	**Mary**^{3} **Swaine**, born 10 Nov 1677. She married **Edward Williams**.
12	ii	**William**^{3} **Swaine**, born 28 Dec 1679; died 4 Jan 1718.
13	iii	**Mehitable**^{3} **Swaine**, born 4 Mar 1683. She married on 21 May 1708 **Robert Rowe**.
14	iv	**John**^{3} **Swaine**, born 16 Jul 1685. He married (1) **Mary Sargent**; (2) **Martha Tongue**.
15	v	**Caleb**^{3} **Swaine**, born 16 Apr 1686.

Second Generation

16 vi Sarah³ **Swaine**, born 25 Nov 1689.
17 vii **Anne³ Swaine**, born 21 Jan 1692.

3. **Sarah² Webster** (Thomas¹), born 21 Jan 1660 in Hampton, Rockingham Co., New Hampshire; died 5 Jan 1745 in Hampton, Rockingham Co., New Hampshire. She married on 21 Jun 1680 in Hampton, Rockingham Co., New Hampshire **William Lane**, born <1657> in <Hampton, Rockingham Co., New Hampshire>; died 14 Feb 1749.

Children of Sarah Webster and William Lane were as follows:

18 i **John³ Lane**, born 17 Feb 1685.
19 ii **Sarah³ Lane**, born 6 Nov 1688.
20 iii **Elizabeth³ Lane**, born 13 Aug 1691.
21 iv **Abigail³ Lane**, born 9 Dec 1693.
22 v **Joshua³ Lane**, born 6 Jun 1696.
23 vi **Samuel³ Lane**, born 4 Aug 1698.
24 vii **Thomas³ Lane**, born 8 Jun 1701.

5. **Thomas² Webster Jr.** (Thomas¹), born 20 Nov 1664 in Hampton, Rockingham Co., New Hampshire; died 7 Mar 1733 in Kingston, Rockingham Co., New Hampshire.[10] He married in Hampton, Rockingham Co., New Hampshire **Sarah Godfrey**, born 26 May 1664 in Hampton,

---

[10] Webster, Prentiss, "One Branch of the Webster Family from Thomas Webster of Ormesby, County Norfolk, England," 1894, Lowell Courier Publishing Company, Lowell, Mass, p. 16.

Second Generation

Rockingham Co., New Hampshire; died 15 Feb 1717 in Kingston, Rockingham Co., New Hampshire, daughter of John Godfrey and Mary Cox.

Moved from Hampton to Kingston between 1710 and 1728.

Children of Thomas Webster Jr. and Sarah Godfrey were as follows:

+ 25   i   **Sarah**^{3} **Webster**, born 9 Sep 1690 in Hampton, Rockingham Co., New Hampshire; died 14 Nov 1710. She married **Samuel Fellows**.

+ 26   ii   **Thomas**^{3} **Webster**, born about 1693 in Hampton, Rockingham Co., New Hampshire; died 13 May 1772 in Kingston, Rockingham Co., New Hampshire. He married (1) **Mary Greeley**; (2) **Elizabeth Ladd**.

27   iii   **Mary**^{3} **Webster**, born 19 May 1696 in Hampton, Rockingham Co., New Hampshire; died 30 Oct 1722 in Kingston, Rockingham Co., New Hampshire. She married on 16 Aug 1716 **John Fifield**, born <1692> in <Kingston, Rockingham Co., New Hampshire>.

28   iv   **Alice**^{3} **Webster**, born 5 Aug 1698 in Hampton, Rockingham Co., New Hampshire; died 30 Oct 1772 in Kingston, Rockingham Co., New Hampshire.

+ 29   v   **Benjamin**^{3} **Webster**, born 24 Aug 1701 in

Second Generation

		Hampton, Rockingham Co., New Hampshire; died 5 Feb 1781 in Kingston, Rockingham Co., New Hampshire. He married (1) **Elizabeth Stuart**; (2) **Mary Stanian**.
30	vi	**Deborah³ Webster**, born 30 Nov 1702 in Hampton, Rockingham Co., New Hampshire; died 2 Feb 1767. She married on 12 Oct 1724 **Zebulon Giddings**.
+ 31	vii	**Joshua³ Webster**, born 2 Sep 1703 in Hampton, Rockingham Co., New Hampshire; died about 1795 in Waterboro, Maine. He married **Abigail Waldron**.
32	viii	**Abigail³ Webster**, born 15 Apr 1706 in Hampton, Rockingham Co., New Hampshire. She married on 25 Dec 1724 **David Quimby**, born 1702 in Kingston, Rockingham Co., New Hampshire.
+ 33	ix	**Deacon Samuel³ Webster**, born 3 Apr 1708 in Hampton, Rockingham Co., New Hampshire; died 1790 in Allenstown, Rockingham Co., New Hampshire. He married (1) **Elizabeth Burnham**; (2) **Dorothy Stancel**.
34	x	**Elizabeth³ Webster**, born 11 Jan 1710 in Hampton, Rockingham Co., New Hampshire. She married on 20 Apr 1731 **Josiah Fowler**, born <1707> in <Kingston, Rockingham Co., New Hampshire>.

Second Generation

6. **Ebenezer² Webster** (Thomas¹), born 1 Aug 1667 in Hampton, Rockingham Co., New Hampshire; died 21 Feb 1756 in Kingston, Rockingham Co., New Hampshire. He married on 25 Jul 1709 in Kingston, Rockingham Co., New Hampshire **Hannah Judkins**, born <1688> in <Kingston, Rockingham Co., New Hampshire>.

Children of Ebenezer Webster and Hannah Judkins were as follows:

+ 35   i   **Ebenezer³ Webster**, born 10 Oct 1714 in Kingston, Rockingham Co., New Hampshire. He married **Susannah Batchelder**.

10. **Abigail² Webster** (Thomas¹), born 1 Jan 1679 in Hampton, Rockingham Co., New Hampshire; died 3 Aug 1758 in Hampton, Rockingham Co., New Hampshire. She married **John Nay**, died 8 Dec 1750 in Hampton, Rockingham Co., New Hampshire.

Children of Abigail Webster and John Nay were as follows:

36   i   **Sarah³ Nay**, born 20 Jun 1705.
37   ii   **Samuel³ Nay**, born 24 Aug 1707.
38   iii   **John³ Nay**, born 16 Aug 1708.
39   iv   **Hannah³ Nay**, born 3 Dec 1710.
40   v   **Ebenezer³ Nay**, christened 19 Jul 1713.
41   vi   **Abigail³ Nay**, christened 19 Jul 1717, died before 1724.

Second Generation

42 vii **Joseph**[3] **Nay**, christened 23 Jul 1722.
43 viii **Abigail**[3] **Nay**, christened 6 Sep 1724

Third Generation

The third generation consists of the Grandchildren of Thomas and Sarah Webster. They were predominately Puritans. They settled the original thirteen colonies and suffered many Indian attacks. They persevered and brought civilization to a harsh land.

25. **Sarah**³ **Webster** (Thomas², Thomas¹), born 9 Sep 1690 in Hampton, Rockingham Co., New Hampshire; died 14 Nov 1710. She married on 14 Nov 1710 **Samuel Fellows**, born 1686 in Kingston, Rockingham Co., New Hampshire; died 12 Oct 1714.

Children of Sarah Webster and Samuel Fellows were as follows:
    44   i   **Samuel**⁴ **Fellows**, born 15 Jun 1712.
    45   ii   **Joseph**⁴ **Fellows**, born 27 Feb 1715.

26. **Thomas**³ **Webster** (Thomas², Thomas¹), born about 1693 in Hampton, Rockingham Co., New Hampshire; died 13 May 1772 in Kingston, Rockingham Co., New Hampshire. He married (1) on 19 Jun 1717 **Mary Greeley**, born 1696 in Kingston, Rockingham Co., New Hampshire; (2) **Elizabeth Ladd**, born 1697 in Kingston, Rockingham Co., New Hampshire.

Children of Thomas Webster and Mary Greeley were as follows:
+   46   i   **Elizabeth**⁴ **Webster**, born 27 Mar 1718;

Third Generation

			died in Newton, New Hampshire. She married **John Carter**.
+	47	ii	**Mary**[4] **Webster**, born 30 Mar 1719; died in South Hampton, New Hampshire. She married **Thomas Carter**.
	48	iii	**Sarah**[4] **Webster**, born 30 Mar 1719.
	49	iv	**Martha**[4] **Webster**, born 16 Jun 1722.
+	50	v	**Alice**[4] **Webster**, born 10 Jan 1724. She married **Jacob Sulloway**.
+	51	vi	**Miriam**[4] **Webster**, born 8 Aug 1729. She married **Philip Davis**.
+	52	vii	**Thomas**[4] **Webster**, born about 1738. He married (1) **(---) Langsford**; (2) **Deborah Lane**.

29. **Benjamin**[3] **Webster** (Thomas[2], Thomas[1]), born 24 Aug 1701 in Hampton, Rockingham Co., New Hampshire; died 5 Feb 1781 in Kingston, Rockingham Co., New Hampshire. He married (1) on 17 Feb 1725 **Elizabeth Stuart**, born 1705 in Kingston, Rockingham Co., New Hampshire, daughter of Ebenezer Stuart and Elizabeth Johnson; (2) on 1 Dec 1737 **Mary Stanian**, born 1716 in Kingston, Rockingham Co., New Hampshire.

Children of Benjamin Webster and Elizabeth Stuart were as follows:

53	i	**Anna**[4] **Webster**, born 17 Oct 1728.
54	ii	**Benjamin**[4] **Webster**, born 8 Dec 1732;

Third Generation

died 22 Nov 1745.

Children of Benjamin Webster and Mary Stanian were as follows:
- 55 i **William**[4] **Webster**, born 22 May 1738; died 11 Nov 1745.
- 56 ii **Elizabeth**[4] **Webster**, born 15 Jun 1740.
- 57 iii **Jacob**[4] **Webster**, born 3 Sep 1742; died 6 Feb 1744.
- + 58 iv **Jacob**[4] **Webster**, born 15 Feb 1744. He married **Elizabeth George**.
- 59 v **Mary**[4] **Webster**, born 30 Sep 1747.
- 60 vi **Dorothy**[4] **Webster**, born 30 Oct 1750.
- 61 vii **Sarah**[4] **Webster**, born 5 Jan 1754.

31. **Joshua**[3] **Webster** (Thomas[2], Thomas[1]), born 2 Sep 1703 in Hampton, Rockingham Co., New Hampshire; died about 1795 in Waterboro, Maine. He married on 7 May 1733 in Kingston, Rockingham Co., New Hampshire **Abigail Waldron**, born <1707> in <Kingston, Rockingham Co., New Hampshire>.

Children of Joshua Webster and Abigail Waldron were as follows:
- 62 i **Samuel**[4] **Webster**, born 28 Jan 1728 in Kingston, Rockingham Co., New Hampshire; died in Waterboro, York County, Maine.

Third Generation

63   ii   **Joshua**[4] **Webster**, born 3 May 1729 in Kingston, Rockingham Co. New Hampshire. He married before 1760 **Mary Watts**, daughter of John Watts.

64   iii   **Abigail**[4] **Webster**, christened 28 Feb 1734, died 1757. She married in 1754 **Stephen Ladd**.

65   iv   **Phebe**[4] **Webster**, born in Kingston, Rockingham Co., New Hampshire; died about 1800 in Waterboro, York County, Maine. She married in 1762 **Stephen Dudley**.

+ 66   v   **Waldron**[4] **Webster**, born about 1741 in Kingston, Rockingham Co., New Hampshire; died about 1803 in Waterboro, York County, Maine. He married **Anna Dudley**.

67   vi   **Benjamin**[4] **Webster**, born about 1741 in Kingston, Rockingham Co., New Hampshire; died in Saco, York County, Maine.

68   vii   **John**[4] **Webster**, born in Kingston, Rockingham Co., New Hampshire; died of palsey 6 Nov 1786 in Saco, York County, Maine.

69   viii   **William**[4] **Webster**, born in Kingston, Rockingham Co., New Hampshire.

70   ix   **Joseph**[4] **Webster**, born 2 Jan 1752 in Kingston, Rockingham Co., New

Hampshire; died 4 Apr 1816 in Saco, York County, Maine. He married in 1785 in Biddeford, Maine **Rhoda Mitchell**.

33. **Deacon Samuel³ Webster** (Thomas², Thomas¹), born 3 Apr 1708 in Hampton, Rockingham Co., New Hampshire; died 1790 in Allenstown, Rockingham Co., New Hampshire.[11] He married (1) on 25 Feb 1733 in Kingston, Rockingham Co., New Hampshire **Elizabeth Burnham**, born 3 Jun 1712 in Kingston, Rockingham Co., New Hampshire; died 20 Oct 1738 in Kingston, Rockingham Co., New Hampshire, daughter of David Burnham and Elizabeth Perkins; (2) in 1740 in Kingston, Rockingham Co., New Hampshire **Dorothy Stancel**, born 1719 in Kingston, Rockingham Co., New Hampshire.

The family lived in Kingston, NH, until the late 1750s, when he either moved or became part of the new parish of Hawke. In the mid 1760s, Samuel³ moved his family to Allenstown, NH, where he eventually died.

The administration of Samuel Webster's estate (Rockingham Probate #5599) was taken by his son, David Webster of Allenstown. Samuel was survived by his widow, Dorothy, who made her mark to documents in his probate. Among the list of claims on his estate were small sums due to "Marey" Webster, John Webster, Dorithy

---

[11] DEATH: Rockingham County Administration Probate #5599.

Third Generation

Webster, Samuel Webster, and Capt. Jacob Webster. By his inventory, Samuel owned property in Allenstown and Chester, NH.

Samuel[3] had three children with his first wife and eleven with his second. Of the children from his second wife, Dorothy, we know of three: Samuel, Joseph, and David. All three of these brothers were Revolutionary War soldiers and fought at the Battle of Bunker Hill. Our line continues through Joseph:

Children of Deacon Samuel Webster and Elizabeth Burnham were as follows:
- 71   i   **Sarah**[4] **Webster**, born 20 Nov 1734 in Kingston, Rockingham Co., New Hampshire; died 25 Jan 1737 in Kingston, Rockingham Co., New Hampshire.
- + 72   ii   **Dorothy**[4] **Webster**, born 10 Sep 1735 in Kingston, Rockingham Co., New Hampshire; died 24 Aug 1805. She married **Jonathan Collins**.
- 73   iii   **Samuel**[4] **Webster**.
- 74   iv   **David**[4] **Webster**, born 30 Sep 1738 in Kingston, Rockingham Co., New Hampshire; died Sep 1757.
- 75   v   **Thomas**[4] **Webster**.

Children of Deacon Samuel Webster and Dorothy Stancel were as follows:

Third Generation

76	i	**Burnham**[4] **Webster**, born 18 Oct 1740; died 8 Nov 1758.
77	ii	**Sarah**[4] **Webster**, born 1 Jan 1742.
78	iii	**Elizabeth**[4] **Webster**, born 11 Jan 1744; died 27 Nov 1751.
79	iv	**Rachel**[4] **Webster**, born 17 Feb 1747; died 22 Nov 1751.
+ 80	v	**Samuel**[4] **Webster**, born 1 Jul 1749 in Kingston, Rockingham Co., New Hampshire; died after 7 Aug 1832 in Tate, Claremont Co., Ohio. He married **Lydia Sargent**.
81	vi	**Rachel**[4] **Webster**, born 7 Dec 1751.
+ 82	vii	**Joseph Stancel**[4] **Webster**, born 2 Apr 1754 in Kingston, Rockingham Co., New Hampshire; died 22 Jul 1837 in Hatley, Quebec, Canada. He married **Mary Carr**.
83	viii	**Elizabeth**[4] **Webster**, born 8 Mar 1756.
+ 84	ix	**David**[4] **Webster**, born 12 Aug 1758 in Hawke, New Hampshire; died 1 Sep 1847 in Colchester, Vermont. He married **Sarah Carr**.
+ 85	x	**Benjamin**[4] **Webster**, born 8 May 1761 in Hawke, New Hampshire. He married **Sarah Page**.
86	xi	**Nanny**[4] **Webster**, born in Hawke, New Hampshire.

Third Generation

35. **Ebenezer³ Webster** (Ebenezer², Thomas¹), born 10 Oct 1714 in Kingston, Rockingham Co., New Hampshire. He married on 20 Jul 1738 in Kingston, New Hampshire **Susannah Batchelder.**

Children of Ebenezer Webster and Susannah Batchelder were as follows:
+ 87 i **Captain Ebenezer⁴ Webster**, born 22 Apr 1739 in Kingston, Rockingham Co., New Hampshire; died 1806 in Salisbury, Merrimack Co., New Hampshire. He married **Abigail Eastman.**

Fourth Generation

The fourth generation is made up of the Great Grandchildren of Thomas and Sarah Webster. They lived in the eighteenth century in the original thirteen colonies. They participated in the French and Indian War and the American Revolutionary War of independence from Great Britain. These were strong, bold people who staked their lives to be free. They defined what it is to be an American through their beliefs and actions.

46. **Elizabeth**[4] **Webster** (Thomas[3], Thomas[2], Thomas[1]), born 27 Mar 1718; died in Newton, New Hampshire. She married **John Carter**, son of John Carter and Judith (---).

Children of Elizabeth Webster and John Carter were as follows:

88	i	**Thomas W.**[5] **Carter**.
89	ii	**John**[5] **Carter**.
90	iii	**Abraham**[5] **Carter**.
91	iv	**Ephraim**[5] **Carter**.
92	v	**Nathaniel**[5] **Carter**.
93	vi	**Elizabeth**[5] **Carter**. She married **Bernard Elliott**.

47. **Mary**[4] **Webster** (Thomas[3], Thomas[2], Thomas[1]), born 30 Mar 1719; died in South Hampton, New Hampshire. She married **Thomas Carter**, son of John Carter and Judith (---).

Fourth Generation

Children of Mary Webster and Thomas Carter were as follows:

- 94   i   **Moses^5 Carter**, born 2 Oct 1739 in South Hampton, New Hampshire.
- 95   ii   **Sarah^5 Carter**, born 21 Jul 1743 in South Hampton, New Hampshire.
- 96   iii   **Mary^5 Carter**, born 2 Jul 1745 in South Hampton, New Hampshire.

50. **Alice^4 Webster** (Thomas^3, Thomas^2, Thomas^1), born 10 Jan 1724. She married on 3 Jun 1748 **Jacob Sulloway**.

Children of Alice Webster and Jacob Sulloway were as follows:

- 97   i   **John^5 Sulloway**, born 23 Jun 1750.
- 98   ii   **Benjamin^5 Sulloway**, born 21 Sep 1752.
- 99   iii   **Jacob^5 Sulloway**, born 11 Dec 1755.
- 100   iv   **Greeley^5 Sulloway**, born 11 Aug 1759.

51. **Miriam^4 Webster** (Thomas^3, Thomas^2, Thomas^1), born 8 Aug 1729. She married **Philip Davis**.

Children of Miriam Webster and Philip Davis were as follows:

- 101   i   **Webster^5 Davis**, born 27 Jul 1751.
- 102   ii   **Marcy^5 Davis**, born 21 Jul 1759.

Fourth Generation

52. **Thomas**[4] **Webster** (Thomas[3], Thomas[2], Thomas[1]), born about 1738. He married (1) **(---) Langsford**, died about 1763, daughter of Richard Langsford and Mary Rowe; (2) **Deborah Lane**.

Children of Thomas Webster and (---) Langsford were as follows:

103 i   **Joshua**[5] **Webster**, born about 1763 in Cape Ann, Glouchester, Massachusetts. He married **Esther Pool**, daughter of Major Mark Pool.

Children of Thomas Webster and Deborah Lane were as follows:

104 i   **Sally**[5] **Webster**, born 1766; died in Bristol, Maine. She married **Joshua Savage**.

58. **Jacob**[4] **Webster** (Benjamin[3], Thomas[2], Thomas[1]), born 15 Feb 1744. He married on 13 Feb 1767 **Elizabeth George**, born 1753; died 13 Mar 1824.

Jacob Webster served in the Revolutionary War as a Captain. See New Hampshire Pension Record #518268.

Children of Jacob Webster and Elizabeth George were as follows:

105 i   **Benjamin**[5] **Webster**, born 31 Jul 1769.
106 ii   **Sarah**[5] **Webster**, born 3 Apr 1771.

Fourth Generation

107   iii   **Polly**[5] **Webster**, born 15 Jun 1774.
108   iv   **Susannah**[5] **Webster**, born 6 Jan 1777.
109   v   **William**[5] **Webster**, born 17 Nov 1779.
110   vi   **John**[5] **Webster**, born 31 May 1782.
111   vii   **Lucy**[5] **Webster**, born 30 Jun 1785.
112   viii   **Nancy**[5] **Webster**, born 20 Aug 1790.

66. **Waldron**[4] **Webster** (Joshua[3], Thomas[2], Thomas[1]), born about 1741 in Kingston, Rockingham Co., New Hampshire; died about 1803 in Waterboro, York County, Maine. He married about 1772 in Brentwood, New Hampshire **Anna Dudley**, born about 1752 in Brentwoods, Rockingham County, New Hampshire; died about 1832 in Waterboro, York County, Maine, daughter of Davison Dudley and Anna Ladd.

Children of Waldron Webster and Anna Dudley were as follows:

113   i   **Sarah**[5] **Webster**, born about 1774 in Waterboro, York County, Maine.
114   ii   **Waldron**[5] **Webster Junior**, born about 1775 in Waterboro, York County, Maine; died after 1830.
115   iii   **Thomas**[5] **Webster**, born about 1777 in Waterboro, York County, Maine; died about 1848 in Waterboro, York County, Maine.
+ 116   iv   **Davison**[5] **Webster**, born 1779 in

Fourth Generation

		Waterboro, York County, Maine; died 16 Feb 1829 in Newfield, York County, Maine. He married **Lucy Drew**.
117	v	**Abigail**[5] **Webster**, born about 1780 in Waterboro, York County, Maine; died after 1800. She married on 29 May 1801 **Trueworthy Chase**.
118	vi	**Anna**[5] **Webster**, born about 1785 in Waterboro, York County, Maine. She married on 18 Feb 1807 in Waterboro, York County, Maine **Stephen Chase**, born about 1778, son of Nathaniel Chase and Margaret Dudley.

72. **Dorothy**[4] **Webster** (Samuel[3], Thomas[2], Thomas[1]), born 10 Sep 1735 in Kingston, Rockingham Co., New Hampshire; died 24 Aug 1805. She married on 29 Apr 1767 **Jonathan Collins**.

Children of Dorothy Webster and Jonathan Collins were as follows:
   119   i   **Samuel**[5] **Collins**.

80. **Samuel**[4] **Webster** (Samuel[3], Thomas[2], Thomas[1]), born 1 Jul 1749 in Kingston, Rockingham Co., New Hampshire; died after 7 Aug 1832 in Tate, Claremont Co., Ohio. He married in 1775 **Lydia Sargent**.

Fourth Generation

Children of Samuel Webster and Lydia Sargent were as follows:

+ 120 i **Burnham^5 Webster**, born 9 Nov 1779; died 23 May 1850 in Indiana. He married **Alice Sargent**.

   121 ii **Samuel^5 Webster**.

82. **Joseph Stancel^4 Webster** (Samuel^3, Thomas^2, Thomas^1), born 2 Apr 1754 in Kingston, Rockingham Co., New Hampshire; died 22 Jul 1837 in Hatley, Quebec, Canada.^{12} He married at Concord, Merrimack County, New Hampshire, 5 June 1777, (NH Vital Records) **Mary Carr**, who is not seen at the time of her husband's death, possibly the daughter of Francis Carr of Bow.^{13}

According to his pension application, Joseph lived in Allenstown, NH around the time of the Revolution. His service is chronicled in the *New Hampshire State Papers* with others from that town, including his brother Samuel. Here is the text of his pension application from the National Archives:

---

^{12} BIRTH: Revolutionary War pension S14810. DEATH: Anglican Church records at Hatley, Canada.

^{13} This information was compiled by Melinde Lutz Sanborn, a researcher in New Hampshire. Joseph's middle name STANCEL was discovered in his muster card records from the Revolutionary War in the National Archives. There were several spellings of the middle name on the muster cards which leads me to believe that it may be close to his mother's maiden name of STANIAN or vice versa.

Fourth Generation

S14810   WEBSTER, JOSEPH
New Hampshire Service

August 14, 1832 Joseph Webster of Hatley, Lower Canada, seventy-eight years of age, deposed:
    that he enlisted the first of May 1775 for eight months, under Capt. Gordon Hutchins, Col. John Stark; went first to Mystic, Mass. where they remained until June 17, when they marched to Bunker Hill; were in that engagement, then went to Winter Hill where they remained until December 1775 when his term having expired he was discharged;
    that in January 1776 he enlisted for two months under Capt. Andrew Buntin, Col. Waldron; were mustered at Temple's farm, near Bunker Hill and served out his two months;
    that the last of May 1778, he enlisted again for two months under Capt. JOSHUA TYLER, and went to cut a road from Newbury, Vt. to St. Johns; served the two months cutting the road as far as Danville, Vt. In June 1777 he enlisted for six months under Capt. Martin, Ensign JAMES MARTIN; marched to Portsmouth, N.H. and was on Pearce's Island about six weeks; then marched to Rhode Island and there completed his term and was discharged;
    that he was born in Kingston, N.H. April 4, 1754; lived in Allenstown, N.H. when he enlisted and he thinks that his entire service was in the New Hampshire Militia.
                         Signed Joseph Webster

Fourth Generation

Witnesses Testimony:

August 15, 1832 EPHRAIM MOORE of Hatley testified to personal knowledge of Joseph Webster serving in 1775; that in the winter of 1775 and 1776 they served together under Capt. Martin near Bunker Hill and later in 1776 they served together under Capt. Tyler, Gen. Bailey, in cutting the road to St. Johns.

                                     Signed by mark

(This application was sworn to at a Probate Court held at Derby, Vt., for Orleans District, Vermont.)

July 23, 1832 DAVID WEBSTER (no place mentioned) asserts that his brother Joseph Webster enlisted the last of April 1775 under Capt. Fletcher, Col. Stark for eight months; that they served together part of the time, and when at home "we sent and received letters from him very frequently;"

that they served together two months in 1776 when the British left Boston, and Gen. Washington marched in triumph into the city;

that after that Joseph served at Rhode Island under Ensign James Martin of Pembrook; who the other officers were he does not remember;

and that he knows that in the winter of 1776 Joseph helped make a road to St. Johns, but does not know the names of any of his officers.

Claim allowed and Certificate 18766, Vermont Agency was issued October 1, 1833 under Act of June 7,

Fourth Generation

1832.

After the Revolution, Joseph married Mary Carr and they settled in Newbury/Fisherfield, New Hampshire, where he was called a gentleman and served as a selectman, an elected town government councilman. Joseph sold two pews in the church at Fisherfield on 11 January 1802 and sold land there in his last Newbury appearance in 1806. He moved sometime between 1806 and 1819 to Hatley, Quebec, Canada, where a few traces of his children, and his death, are recorded. The availability of good land in lower Quebec motivated many to move there at that time.

Joseph and Mary (Carr) Webster had ten known children. Their second child is believed to be my Third Great Grandfather, Samuel Webster:

Children of Joseph Stancel Webster and Mary Carr were as follows:

 122 i   **Sarah^5 Webster**, born 28 Aug 1777 in Allenstown, New Hampshire.
+ 123 ii   **Samuel^5 Webster**, born 23 Nov 1778 in Fisherfield, Merrimack Co., New Hampshire; died 16 Jan 1847 in York Twp, Noble Co., Indiana. He married **Deborah Fuller**.
 124 iii **Joseph^5 Webster**, born 28 Mar 1781 in Fisherfield, Merrimack Co., New Hampshire.
 125 iv   **David^5 Webster**, born 18 Apr 1783 in

Fourth Generation

		Fisherfield, Merrimack Co., New Hampshire.
126	v	**Polly**[5] **Webster**, born 18 Jan 1785 in Fisherfield, Merrimack Co., New Hampshire.
127	vi	**John**[5] **Webster**, born 7 Apr 1787 in Fisherfield, Merrimack Co., New Hampshire.
128	vii	**Ruth**[5] **Webster**, born 9 Apr 1790 in Fisherfield, Merrimack Co., New Hampshire.
129	viii	**Bety**[5] **Webster**, born 21 May 1792 in Fisherfield, Merrimack Co., New Hampshire.
+ 130	ix	**Francis**[5] **Webster**, born 20 Jul 1794 in Fisherfield, Merrimack Co., New Hampshire. He married **Nancy Whitcomb**.
131	x	**Lydia**[5] **Webster**, born 25 Jun 1796 in Fisherfield, Merrimack Co., New Hampshire.

84. **David**[4] **Webster** (Samuel[3], Thomas[2], Thomas[1]), born 12 Aug 1758 in Hawke, New Hampshire; died 1 Sep 1847 in Colchester, Vermont. He married **Sarah Carr**, born 1762 in Hawke, New Hampshire; died 1847 in Colchester, Vermont.

David Webster was a Revolutionary War pensioner. See New Hampshire Pension Record #S15699.

Fourth Generation

Children of David Webster and Sarah Carr were as follows:
- 132 i **Thomas Carr**[5] **Webster**, born 1801; died 1864. He married **Julia Ann** (---).

85. **Benjamin**[4] **Webster** (Samuel[3], Thomas[2], Thomas[1]), born 8 May 1761 in Hawke, New Hampshire. He married on 25 Apr 1785 **Sarah Page**, died 4 Jun 1809 in Kingston, Rockingham Co., New Hampshire, daughter of Thomas Page and Mary Elkins.

Children of Benjamin Webster and Sarah Page were as follows:
- 133 i **Nathaniel**[5] **Webster**, died in Danville, New Hampshire.
- 134 ii **Henry**[5] **Webster**, died in Appleton, Maine.
- 135 iii **Jacob**[5] **Webster**.
- 136 iv **Thomas**[5] **Webster**, born 7 May 1787; died in Appleton, Maine.
- 137 v **Benjamin**[5] **Webster**, died in Appleton, Maine.
- 138 vi **Martha**[5] **Webster**, died in Appleton, Maine.
- 139 vii **Eliza**[5] **Webster**, died in Appleton, Maine.

87. **Captain Ebenezer**[4] **Webster** (Ebenezer[3], Ebenezer[2],

Fourth Generation

Thomas[1]), born 22 Apr 1739 in Kingston, Rockingham Co., New Hampshire; died 1806 in Salisbury, Merrimack Co., New Hampshire. He married **Abigail Eastman**.

Captain Ebenezer Webster was a distinguished soldier in the French and Indian War and the Revolutionary War.

Children of Ebenezer Webster Captain and Abigail Eastman were as follows:

140   i   **Senator Daniel[5] Webster**, born 18 Jan 1782; died 24 Oct 1852. This is the famous U.S. Senator and Secretary of State. He married (1) **Grace Fletcher**, who died Jan 1828, (2) **Caroline LeRoy** in Dec 1829.

Fifth Generation

The members of the fifth generation were the Great Great Grandchildren of Thomas and Sarah Webster. They were born when our republic was still in its infancy. They experienced the War of 1812 and Indian Wars. Many lived on to see the Civil War. They also started pushing the frontiers westward. These people were tough pioneers and were motivated by the desire to obtain their own land.

116. **Davison**[5] **Webster** (Waldron[4], Joshua[3], Thomas[2], Thomas[1]), born 1779 in Waterboro, York County, Maine; died 16 Feb 1829 in Newfield, York County, Maine. He married on 5 Jul 1801 in Newfield, Maine **Lucy Drew**, born 13 Sep 1786 in Madbury, New Hampshire; died 22 May 1869 in Newfield, Maine, daughter of Elijah Drew and Lucy (---). Davison Webster was a blacksmith.

Children of Davison Webster and Lucy Drew were as follows:

- 141   i   **Elizabeth**[6] **Webster**, born 22 Feb 1803 in Newfield, Maine.
- 142   ii   **Lois**[6] **Webster**, born 13 Dec 1804; died 27 Sep 1876 in Newfield, Maine.
- + 143 iii **Baker**[6] **Webster**, born 5 Mar 1807 in Newfield, Maine; died 3 Oct 1868 in Fort Dodge, Iowa. He married **Louisana** (---).
- 144   iv   **Benjamin**[6] **Webster**, died in Portsmouth, Rockingham County, New Hampshire. He married on 7 Apr 1809 **Lyn** (---).
- 145   v   **Davison**[6] **Webster**, born 30 Apr 1811 in

Fifth Generation

Waterboro, York County, Maine; died 7 Jan 1844 in Portsmouth, Rockingham County, New Hampshire. He married on 30 Nov 1834 **Julia Ann Dearborn**, born 27 Nov 1806 in Portsmouth, Rockingham County, New Hampshire.

146   vi   **Lucy**[6] **Webster**, born 24 Dec 1813.
147   vii   **Abigail**[6] **Webster**, born 12 May 1816.
148   viii   **John**[6] **Webster**, born 25 Nov 1818; died 5 Jul 1820.
149   ix   **John**[6] **Webster**, born 27 May 1821. He married **Sarah Perry**.

120. **Burnham**[5] **Webster** (Samuel[4], Samuel[3], Thomas[2], Thomas[1]), born 9 Nov 1779; died 23 May 1850 in Indiana. He married on 21 Dec 1804 **Alice Sargent**, died 18 Sep 1821 in Waterville, Maine.

Children of Burnham Webster and Alice Sargent were as follows:

150   i   **Patty**[6] **Webster**, born 8 Sep 1806 in Waterville, Maine.
151   ii   **Minerva**[6] **Webster**, born 16 Dec 1807 in Waterville, Maine; died 21 Jan 1866.
152   iii   **Leander**[6] **Webster**, born 12 Apr 1809 in Waterville, Maine; died 19 May 1895.
153   iv   **Auristella**[6] **Webster**, born 2 Sep 1811 in Waterville, Maine; died 22 Jun 1866. She

Fifth Generation

    married **Benjamin Denham**.
154 v **Starlin S.**⁶ **Webster**, born 6 Feb 1813 in Waterville, Maine.
155 vi **David F.**⁶ **Webster**, born 10 Feb 1815.

123. **Samuel**⁵ **Webster** (Joseph Stancel⁴, Samuel³, Thomas², Thomas¹), born 23 Nov 1778 in Fisherfield, Merrimack Co., New Hampshire (recorded Newbury, NH); died 16 Jan 1847 in York Twp, Noble Co., Indiana. He married on 16 Jul 1809 in Wheelock, Caledonia Co., Vermont **Deborah Fuller**¹⁴, born about 1790 (calculated from census) in Dartmouth, Bristol Co., Massachusetts¹⁵; died 24 Jun 1849 in Ottawa Co., Ohio¹⁶, daughter of

---

¹⁴ Howard Webster discovered the wedding record of Samuel and Deborah Webster by hiring a researcher to find it in the Vermont Vital Records.

¹⁵ BIRTH: Deborah's birth was derived from her death record that says she was born in Vermont. The birth dates of her children come from the back of an account book probably maintained by David Webster. However, other evidence indicates that Deborah may have been born in Massachusetts and moved to Vermont at a very early age. So she may have thought she was born in Vermont since she grew up there and did not know any other place. Also, her children, who gave the information for the death certificate, may have mistakenly assumed that she was born in Vermont.

¹⁶ DEATH: Deborah Webster's death records where found in a book entitled "Mortality Schedule Ohio 1850" at the National Archives. Our family records had her death on 24 June 1849, but the book listing provided her age and birth place. Her cause of death was listed as Erysipedas, an acute streptococcus bacteria disease of the

Fifth Generation

Simeon Fuller and Anna Blackmer.

Samuel[5] is believed to be the son of Joseph.[4] Here is one of the two points where we do not have a solid connection. However, even though the evidence we have is mostly circumstantial, a preponderance of circumstantial evidence is proof enough to support the lineage in the absence of evidence to the contrary, and there is none of that. This type of evidence is probably all we can hope for from that period. The evidence is grouped into five areas:

    a.   **The age of Samuel**, the son of Joseph and Mary Webster of Fisherfield, does agree with census records for the age of my Samuel. This connection is even stronger when the relatively unusual fact is considered that my Samuel is about 12 years older than Deborah.

    b.   **The time and route of Joseph's move** from New Hampshire to Canada coincides with Samuel's appearance in Wheelock. It is conceivable that Joseph's family stopped along the main road they must have taken through Caledonia County, Vermont and visited the group of Websters in Cabot, Vermont on their way to Canada. The Cabot Websters were also from the same New Hampshire Thomas Webster line as Joseph. So they may have been close relatives and kept in touch. Samuel met Deborah in nearby Wheelock and decided to stay on.

---

skin. She was living with her daughter, Nancy Lindsey (later Green) at the time.

Fifth Generation

c. **Vermont was the logical progression west** from New Hampshire, and west was the predominant migration direction for most pioneers.

d. **The consistency of the names** between generations fits very well. This is especially true for the naming convention of the first son being named for the father of the husband.

e. **Our family lore** that says we are distant cousins of Daniel Webster fits as well.

The 1810 Census shows Samuel[5] and Deborah (Fuller) Webster in Wheelock, Vermont with their first born son, Joseph. Wheelock is in Caledonia County. The word "Caledonia" is the Roman name for Scotland. Vermont history shows that the first settlers of the Wheelock area were predominantly Scottish immigrants in 1773. The Webster name can be found in southern Scotland and is a member of the MacFarlane clan.

The early 1800s was a difficult time in this part of the country. The climate was in a period called the Little Ice Age. The growing season that far north was very short. The mountainous, rocky, forested land was difficult to clear and did not make good farms. In addition, during the War of 1812, smuggling and hostilities became so bad along the Canadian border that northern Vermont was evacuated.[17]

---

[17] Eichholz, Alice, Collecting Vermont Ancestors, New Trails!, 1993,

Fifth Generation

There was plenty of motivation for Samuel and Deborah to move on to better and safer farming land west.

Although I could not specifically find Samuel and Deborah in the 1820 Census in New York, Ohio, or Kentucky, there was a concentration of Websters, Carrs, and Fullers in Onondaga County, New York. Extended families tended to migrate together. Samuel's family may have been living in an older relative's household and therefore were not counted separately. Also, there is a town in Onondaga County named Manlius, which may explain the unusual name of their second son, Manly. Their twin boys, John, my second Great Grandfather, and David and their fifth son, Simeon, were born in New York as well.

There is a curious ten year gap in the children's births, then were born their last know children, twin girls, Nancy O. and Mary Jane, in Kentucky in 1826. We do not know the location in Kentucky.

Montpelier, page 12.

Fifth Generation

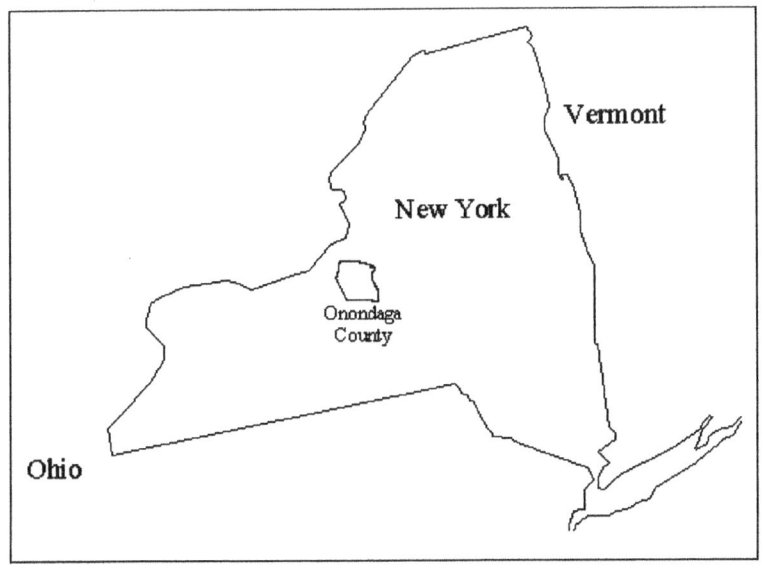

Figure 2 – Map of New York state showing relevant points.

Samuel and Deborah clearly show up in Union Township, Ross County, Ohio in the 1830 Census with John and David Webster families nearby. Again, there was a concentration of Websters and Carrs in adjoining Ross and Fayette Counties in Ohio. The United States was selling Ohio land for $2 per acre through Federal Land Offices.

At about 1838, Samuel, a pioneer still pushing west, accompanied his youngest son, Simeon, to York Township, Noble County, Indiana, where the two men appear in the 1840 Census, both engaged in agriculture. It is likely that

Fifth Generation

Samuel died in Noble County about seven years later.[18]

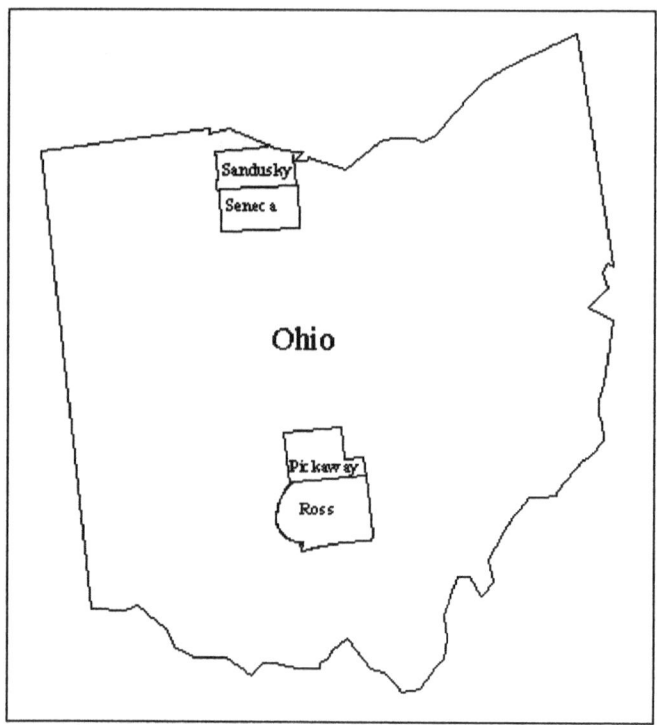

Figure 3 – Map of Ohio showing relevant points.

---

[18] Bernice Webster, Howard's widow, wrote to me on Nov 19, 1991 that "Simeon Webster, John Webster's brother, went with his father, Samuel, and was one of the six earliest settlers in York Township, Noble County, Indiana, being there about 1838. We do not know if Samuel Webster stayed on there until his death on Jan 16, 1847 or not." Bernice said she and Howard tried to find a will but were told the Noble County Court House records had been destroyed by fire.

Fifth Generation

Bernice Webster, Howard's widow, wrote to me on Nov 19, 1991 that "Simeon Webster, John Webster's brother, went with his father, Samuel, and was one of the six earliest settlers in York Township, Noble County, Indiana, being there about 1838. We do not know if Samuel Webster stayed on there until his death on Jan 16, 1847 or not."

Bernice said she and Howard tried to find a will but were told the Noble County Court House records had been destroyed by fire.

Record of movement of Samuel and Deborah Webster and their family:
    Jul 16, 1809 - 1810 - Wheelock, Vermont
In Alice Eichholz book, "Collecting Vermont Relatives," she says on page 12 that there was much lawlessness and danger during the War of 1812 and northern Vermont towns were evacuated. This may be the motivation for Samuel and Deborah moving west. From verified birth records of their children, we can place the family at these locations at these times:
1814 - New York State
1820 - Could not conclusively locate in New York, Ohio, or Kentucky in Census.
1826 - Kentucky
1830 - Union Township, Ross County, Ohio (1830 Census, p 221)
1838 - York Township, Noble County, Indiana

Fifth Generation

1840 - Sandusky or Seneca County, Ohio (1840 Census shows Samuel and his son, Simeon, at York Township, Noble County, Indiana).

Children of Samuel Webster and Deborah Fuller were as follows:

- 156 i **Joseph⁶ Webster**, born 16 Jun 1810 in Wheelock Twp., Caledonia Co., Vermont. Notes: The 1810 census shows Samuel and Deborah with one child in Wheelock, Vermont.
- 157 ii **Manly⁶ Webster**, born 14 Oct 1811 in Wheelock, Caledonia Co., Vermont.
- + 158 iii **John H.⁶ Webster**, born 4 Feb 1814 in New York; died 15 Mar 1876 in Green Twp., Iowa Co., Iowa. He married **Mary Magdalene Moomey**.
- + 159 iv **David⁶ Webster**, born 4 Feb 1814 in New York; died 1 Jan 1893 in Green Twp., Iowa Co., Iowa. He married **Ann Elizabeth Teatsworth**.
- + 160 v **Simeon⁶ Webster**, born 11 Apr 1816 in New York. He married (1) **Polly A. DePew**; (2) **Rhoda (---)**.
- + 161 vi **Nancy O.⁶ Webster**, born 14 Feb 1826 in Kentucky; died 1888 in Washington Co., Kansas. She married (1) **Elihu Lindsey**; (2) **Lyman Green**.
- 162 vii **Mary Jane⁶ Webster**, born 14 Feb 1826 in Kentucky; died 22 Apr 1841 in Ohio.

Fifth Generation

Deborah Fuller Webster is a very significant person in this genealogy. She was the line carrier of five known Mayflower Pilgrim ancestors. These lines consist of some of the most illustrious of the Mayflower Pilgrims: Doctor Samuel Fuller, the deacon and physician of the Pilgrims; Captain Myles Standish, the military commander of the Pilgrims; John Alden and Priscilla Mullins, the young lovers made famous by the poet Henry Wadsworth Longfellow in "The Courtship of Miles Standish"; and the orphan Henry Samson.

This link to the Mayflower Pilgrims was discovered by Dr. Alice Eichholz of Vermont and was developed by Alicia Williams, the Editor of *The Mayflower Descendant*, the official scholarly journal of the Mayflower Society.

Both of Deborah Fuller's parents are Mayflower Pilgrim line carriers. However, this is the second place where a great deal of circumstantial evidence combined to support claims of lineage. A respected genealogy of the Mayflower Pilgrim Doctor Samuel Fuller listed a Simeon Fuller similar to Deborah's father, but the genealogy lost track of him and had no death information at all. The task was to prove that Deborah's father, Simeon, was the one and only Simeon in Doctor Samuel Fuller's genealogy. The dates and other facts pointed in that direction. Dr. Alice Eichholz found a key fact. In Deborah's father's will, a son with the unusual name of Ziba is listed. It was found that the Simeon Fuller in Dr. Fuller's genealogy also had a son named Ziba of consistent age. Alicia Williams pulled together this fact and other evidence into an article for *The Mayflower Descendant* and that invited comment from other researchers.[19] There were no facts to the contrary submitted by anyone. Official publication of the evidence led to approval of my application for membership in the Society of Mayflower Descendants and its validation of my lineage to Doctor Samuel Fuller.[20]

The genealogies of our Mayflower Pilgrims are well documented in other books, so there is no need for an exhaustive accounting of them here. I will just capsulate their stories and our descent from them.

As discussed in the introduction to this part, the Pilgrims were Separatists who wanted to separate from the Church of England and its hierarchy to worship as they wanted. This freedom was not allowed in England at the time, so the Separatists escaped to the Netherlands, which had a truce in its religious war with Catholic Spain and where religious tolerance was practiced. They went first to Amsterdam in

---

[19] Williams, Alicia, Lost: Did Simeon5 Fuller (Samuel,4 John,3 Samuel2-1) marry Ann6 Blackmer (Rebecca5 Samson, Penelope3 Samson, James,3 Henry1) and settle in Dartmouth, New Bedford, and Vermont?, *The Mayflower Descendant*, Vol. 42, No. 2, 2 July 1992, Massachusetts Society of Mayflower Descendants, Boston, Massachusetts, pages 178-180.

[20] My General Number in the Society of Mayflower Descendants is 58910 for reference to those who want to piggy-back on my evidence to gain membership.

1608 and then in 1609 to the university city of Leyden. However, after twelve years, the truce with Spain was due to end perhaps along with their religious freedom. In addition, the Separatists found it difficult to make a living in a foreign country, and their children were becoming Dutch instead of English. All these factors motivated them to move to the New World.[21] Some settlements of adventurers, such as Jamestown, had already been established, but no settlements involving families had succeeded.

The Separatists found merchant sponsors and hired people with skills they did not have. They hired a ship called the Mayflower and bought a ship called the Speedwell. The Speedwell proved unseaworthy, so the group loaded as many as possible, 102 souls, on the Mayflower and made the voyage in the fall of 1620. They explored the Cape Cod area and finally settled by a natural bay they called Plymouth after their departure point in England. The Pilgrims were not well prepared and came too late in the year to complete their houses before winter, so most of them lived on the ship until spring. The winter was so harsh that only half their number survived to see spring, but the rest went on to establish a great colony and American customs that live on and are remembered every Thanksgiving Day. Now, we will review each of the five Mayflower Pilgrim ancestors in our family:

---

[21] Steketee, John W., "The Pilgrims in Leyden," *The Mayflower Quarterly*, Vol. 60 No. 3, August 1994, The General Society of Mayflower Descendants, Plymouth, Massachusetts, pages 187-195.

First is Doctor Samuel Fuller who was born the son of Robert and Sarah (Dunthorne) Fuller at Redenhall Parish, Harleston, Norfolk County, England, 20 January 1580.[22] We know of five generations prior to Samuel at Redenhall Parish.[23] There is no physical description of Samuel Fuller. He was a physician and surgeon educated at Cambridge University. Samuel was a fervent Separatist and was the leader of a group of English religious exiles that merged with the main Pilgrim group in 1608 in Amsterdam. His brother, Edward Fuller, a lawyer, and his family accompanied the Separatists on the Mayflower but died in the first winter. Edward is believed to have written the Mayflower Compact, the historic and precedent setting democratic governing document, which he and Samuel signed. Samuel was a tender-hearted man who cared for the other Pilgrims during that terrible first winter and was instrumental with making friends of the Native Americans and later of the Puritans of the Massachusetts Bay Colony through his medical treatment. He raised several orphans and was a trusted advisor to the governors of Plymouth Colony until his death in 1633.

Doctor Samuel Fuller was married three times. Our line comes from his third wife, Bridget Lee, daughter of Josephine Lee. Samuel and Bridget were married at

---

[22] Mary, Lucy, Ed., Mayflower Families Through Five Generations, Vol. One, General Society of Mayflower Descendants, 1975, Plymouth, Massachusetts, pages 49-92.

[23] Butler, Jean Fuller, A History of the Fuller Family and Other Collateral Lines, Self Published, Found at DAR Library, page 174.

Leyden, 27 May 1617. Bridget followed her husband to Plymouth in 1623 arriving on the ship "Anne." We descend from their third child, Samuel[2]; then his son, John[3]; then his son, Samuel[4]; and finally Deborah's father, Simeon[5]. Today the Fuller Society seeks to keep the memory of Doctor Fuller and his brother alive and expand knowledge of the ancestors and descendants.

Second is Captain Myles Standish who was born on The Isle of Man about 1584.[24] He was described as being short and stout with red hair and a ruddy complexion. Myles was a British soldier in the Netherlands keeping the truce with Spain and became acquainted with the Separatist group in Leyden. He was retained by them as their military leader, came with them to New England, and served in that function until his death in 1656. He had several courageous run-ins with the local Native Americans but was able to keep the peace most of the time. A signer of the Mayflower Compact, he also served several times as Assistant Governor of Plymouth Colony. His first wife, Rose, accompanied him on the Mayflower but died the first winter. Myles and Rose are depicted in the Robert Weir painting "Embarkation of the Pilgrims" hanging in the U.S. Capitol Rotunda. His second wife, Barbara, from whom we descend, came over on the ship "Anne" in 1623 and married Myles at Plymouth. It is believed she was a sort of mail

---

[24] Warner, Russell L., *Mayflower Families in Progress - Myles Standish of the Mayflower and His Descendants for Five Generations*, General Society of Mayflower Descendants, 1992, Plymouth, Massachusetts, page 1.

order bride. They were given land in Duxbury across Plymouth harbor in 1627 and moved there permanently in 1632. A towering monument to Myles Standish overlooks the Plymouth harbor from Duxbury today. Myles and Barbara had seven children. We descend from their second child, Alexander[2]; then his daughter, Lora[3] (Standish) Sampson; then her son, Abraham[4] Sampson; his daughter, Rebecca[5] (Samson) Blackmer; and finally Deborah's mother, Anna[6] (Blackmer) Fuller.

Third is John Alden who was born possibly at Southampton, Hampshire County, England before 12 September 1598.[25] He is described as being tall, blonde, and very strong. He was a 21 year old cooper and was hired by the Pilgrims to tend their barrels of beer, wine, and strong waters and to help in the construction of their houses. It is believed he was related by marriage to Christopher Jones, the master and part owner of the Mayflower, and that Master Jones may have been instrumental in getting John Alden the job.[26] William Bradford wrote of him in his *History of Plymouth Plantation*, "John Alden was hired for a cooper at Southampton wher the ship was victuled, and being a hopefull youngman was much desired, but left to

---

[25] Drummond, Audrey and Nancy J. Springer, *Mayflower Passengers 1620*, Massachusetts Society of Mayflower Descendants, 1992, Boston, page 3.

[26] Williams, Alicia Crane, "John Alden: Theories on English Ancestry," The Mayflower Descendant, Vol. 40, No. 2, 2 July 1990, Massachusetts Society of Mayflower Descendants, Boston, pages 133-136.

his owne liking to go, or stay when he came here, but he stayed, and maryed here."(sic) In 1623, he married Priscilla Mullins who at about sixteen lost both of her parents in the first winter. A signer of the Mayflower Compact, John Alden served several times as Assistant Governor, deputy to the General Court, treasurer, deputy governor, and on various committees including councils of war against the Dutch and Indians.[27] Like the Standishes, the Aldens were granted land in Duxbury in 1627 and moved there permanently in 1632. Their second house in Duxbury built in 1653 still stands and is a museum today operated by the Alden Kindred of America.[28] John Alden was very robust all his life and died in 1687 at age 89. Priscilla died sometime before John. They had ten children. We descend from their fourth child, Sarah[2], who married Alexander[2] Standish; then their daughter, Lora[3] (Standish) Sampson; then her son, Abraham[4] Sampson; his daughter, Rebecca[5] (Samson) Blackmer; and finally Deborah's mother, Anna[6] (Blackmer) Fuller.

Fourth is William Mullins, who was born the son of John and Joane (Bridger) Mullyns at Dorking, Surrey County,

---

[27] Shaw, Hubert K. and Alicia Crane Williams, *Families of the Pilgrims - John Alden and William Mullins*, Massachusetts Society of Mayflower Descendants, 1986, Boston, page 1.

[28] Approval of my application for membership in the Alden Kindred of America validates my lineage to the John Alden, Priscilla Mullins, William Mullins, Myles Standish, and Henry Samson. For those of you who want to piggy-back on my application, the number of the file is ACW-642.

England, about 1572, and died with his wife, Alice, the first winter at Plymouth Colony about 21 February 1621.[29] He was a well-to-do cordwainer (leatherworker) and shopkeeper in Dorking where he sold boots and shoes. He was also a religious dissenter in sympathy with the Separatists. William and Alice had four known children. We are descended from their third child, Priscilla, who married John Alden.

Fifth is Henry Samson who was born the son of James and Martha (Cooper) Samson at Henlow, Bedford County, England, 15 January 1603 or 1604.[30] He was an orphan and accompanied his cousins, Edward and Ann Tilley, on the Mayflower when he was in his late teens. He married Ann Plummer at Plymouth in 1635, and they had nine children. Henry died at Duxbury in 1684. We are descended from Henry[1] and Ann's seventh child, James[2]; then his daughter, Penelope[3] (Samson) Sampson; then her daughter, Rebecca[4] (Samson) Blackmer; and finally Deborah's mother, Anna[5] (Blackmer) Fuller.

We may have more Mayflower ancestors, because the Pilgrims lived in close proximity to each other for almost

---

[29] Williams, Alicia Crane, "The Mullins Family," *The Mayflower Descendant* Vol 44, No 1, January 1994, Massachusetts Society of Mayflower Descendants, Boston, pages 39-44.

[30] Sherman, Robert and Ruth, Mayflower Families in Progress - Henry Samson of the Mayflower and His Descendants for Four Generations, General Society of Mayflower Descendants, 1992, Plymouth, Massachusetts, page 4.

two hundred years and there was much intermarrying. However, our lineage from these five very significant Pilgrims is known to us now but perhaps more will surface later.

Before we leave Deborah Fuller's line, her father, Simeon, deserves some attention. He was quite a character. There are records showing he caused a disturbance at church when he was 17 years old.[31] Then six years later Anna Blackmer jilted her fiance to marry Simeon.[32]

However, the most significant story about Simeon Fuller is his Revolutionary War service. My research of it was the basis for my successful application to membership in the Sons of the American Revolution (SAR).[33] I wrote an article about Simeon's service that was published in the Fall 1993 Virginia Bulletin of the SAR. Here is the text of that article:

The Revolutionary War Service of Simeon Fuller of Dartmouth, Massachusetts

by Dale Douglas Webster, his Fourth Great Grandson

---

[31] "Found," *The Mayflower Descendant*, July 1993, Massachusetts Society of Mayflower Descendants, Boston, page 9.

[32] Vital Records, Dartmouth, Massachusetts.

[33] For those of you who want to piggy-back on my application to the SAR, the file number is 140479.

Simeon Fuller of Dartmouth, Massachusetts served for a significant period and in major battles of the American Revolutionary War. Evidence of his service was compiled by comparing his war records from the National Archives with published accounts of the Revolutionary War. His war records are in the form of muster cards that give his unit, location, date, and other sketchy details at several times during his service. By looking up the exploits of his officers, descriptions of battles, and the arrangements of units on the battlefield, it is possible to match them with his war records and tell with reasonable certainty what Simeon did during the War. This brief article describes the results of that analysis.

He was born in Middleboro, Massachusetts on September 13, 1741 and was a Second Great Grandson of Doctor Samuel Fuller of the Mayflower.[34] Simeon married Anna Blackmer on October 6, 1764 and established their household in her hometown of Dartmouth, Massachusetts.[35] Simeon was a tailor by trade, stood five feet and nine inches tall, and had a light complexion and dark hair.[36]

---

[34] Kellogg, Mary Lucy, Mayflower Families Through Five Generations, Volume One, (General Society of Mayflower Descendants, Plymouth, Massachusetts, 1975), page 74.

[35] "Lost Article, The Mayflower Descendant, Volume 42, No. 2, 2 July 1992, pages 178-180.

[36] Secretary of the Commonwealth, Massachusetts Soldiers and Sailors of the Revolutionary War, Volume 6, (Wright and Potter Printing County, London, 1899), page 186.

Lexington and Concord

Simeon Fuller's Revolutionary War service began by enlisting as a Private and Drummer in Captain Thomas Kempton's Company of Minutemen, Colonel Timothy Danielson's Regiment[37] of the Massachusetts Militia, on April 21, 1775 in response to the alarm of April 19, 1775 made famous by the ride of Paul Revere.[38] The British marched from Boston to Concord, Massachusetts to capture arms the rebels had stored there. The first shots of the War were fired at Lexington on the way to Concord. Simeon served five days, and, according to his regimental commander's records, his unit was engaged in some skirmishes with the British.[39]

The Battle of Bunker Hill

The rebellious activities continued in Boston, and the British sent for more troops from England to occupy the city. In response to this action, Simeon was again called to active service in the same unit two weeks later on May 4, 1775. Colonel Danielson's records show that the regiment

---

[37] A company was usually commanded by a captain and consisted of about 100 soldiers. A regiment was commanded by a colonel and consisted of about eight companies. There were three to four regiments to a brigade which was commanded by a brigadier general.

[38] Massachusetts Soldiers and Sailors, Volume 6, page 186.

[39] Ibid, Volume 4, page 417.

marched to Roxbury, Massachusetts just outside of Boston and remained there for about three months.[40] Tensions increased until a showdown resulted between Colonial and British forces on June 17, 1775 at Breed's Hill and Bunker Hill north of Boston.

Simeon's unit was part of the right wing under General Thomas that encircled the city.[41] The right wing's mission was to reinforce forces at Bunker Hill and hold the high ground of Dorchester Heights that strategically overlooked Boston. During the battle, the right wing fell under furious cannonade from British warships in the harbor. The battle ended in a standoff with the British maintaining their occupation of Boston and the Colonials still encircling the city.

Meanwhile, in Philadelphia, the Continental Congress commissioned George Washington to become Commander-In-Chief of the Continental Army that still had to be raised. Washington left Philadelphia on June 21st and arrived at the main camp of the encirclement forces at Cambridge on July 2nd. The next day, July 3rd, all the Colonial forces were assembled for the ceremony in which Washington took command.[42] Simeon no doubt witnessed it. Afterwards, Washington concentrated on raising the

---

[40] Ibid.

[41] Lossing, Benson J, The Pictorial Field-Book of the Revolution, (Charles E. Tuttle Company, Rutland, Vermont, 1972), page 537.

[42] Ibid, page 554.

Continental Army, training it, and fortifying the American encirclement of Boston. At the end of July, Simeon went home with his unit and returned to normal life.

The Siege of Boston

In order to take Boston, Washington needed firepower, so he sent Henry Knox to take artillery from the captured British Fort Ticonderoga in upper New York. The 50 large cannons at the fort were dragged by oxen over snow and ice in the winter to Boston. They arrived in February, 1776.[43] Washington deployed them on Dorchester Heights which dominated the Boston area.

At the same time, Washington asked for a show of force from the militia. Simeon Fuller's records show he again responded. He was put in Captain Benjamin Dillingham's Company of Colonel Jacob French's Regiment of the Massachusetts Militia.[44] He arrived in the Boston area on February 15, 1776 and camped at Winter Hill, which is just west of Bunker Hill. On March 17, 1776, the British Army evacuated Boston and went to New York City.[45]

Simeon's unit remained on active duty defending the

---

[43] McDowell, Bart, The Revolutionary War, (National Geographic Society, Washington, DC, 1972), pages 57 and 75.

[44] Massachusetts Soldiers and Sailors, Volume 4, page 773 and Volume 6, page 186.

[45] McDowell, The Revolutionary War, page 77.

seacoast around Dartmouth until November, 1776.

At this same time, General Washington took his Continental Army to engage the British in New York and New Jersey. However, things did not go well for the Americans. Washington had minor victories at Trenton and Princeton but lost at Fort Lee and Brandywine. The British took Philadelphia, and Washington retreated to eastern Pennsylvania.[46]

On July 19, 1777, Simeon Fuller went to Boston and enlisted as a Private in the Continental Army. He was put in Captain James Jones's Company in the 16th Regiment commanded by Colonel Henry Jackson.[47] He trained at the American fort at Dorchester Heights in Boston until early October.

Meanwhile, British General Burgoyne attempted to cut the colonies in half. His plan was to march his British forces south from Canada down the Hudson Valley, occupy it all the way to New York City, and thus cut New England off from the southern colonies. Divide and conquer.

A large American force of three brigades under the command of General Horatio Gates was waiting for Burgoyne's army on the north bank of the Hudson River

---

[46] Grun, Bernard, The Timetables of History, (Simon and Schuster, New York, 1979), page 360.

[47] Muster cards for Simeon Fuller of Dartmouth, Massachusetts on record at the National Archives in Washington, DC.

Deborah Fuller Webster and Her Ancestors

near Albany in Saratoga County.[48]

The Battle of Saratoga occurred on October 17, 1777, and the Americans won decisively. Burgoyne surrendered the next day. The Battle of Saratoga is considered a very important turning point in the war, because this victory motivated France to enter the war on the American side.[49]

Valley Forge

In the late fall of 1777, Simeon's unit joined General Washington's forces and wintered in Pennsylvania. Washington selected Valley Forge as a good defendable site that was big enough to allow his forces to train and was close enough to observe the British at Philadelphia. Simeon's regiment is listed on the Massachusetts Military Monument at Valley Forge, Pennsylvania as having been in the camp during that horrible winter of 1777-78 in which many died of cold, disease, hunger, and despair.[50] Washington's forces dropped from 12,000 strong to 6,000 during the winter. Simeon's muster card for December, 1777 says he was sick with smallpox, which reached epidemic proportions at Valley Forge. The cards for the following three months show him to be in Lancaster,

---

[48] Lossing, Pictorial Field-Book, Volume 1, page 51.

[49] McDowell, The Revolutionary War, page 121.

[50] Reade, Brigadier-General Philip, Dedication Exercises at the Massachusetts Military Monument Valley Forge, PA, (Wright and Potter Printing Company, Boston, 1912), page 23.

Pennsylvania, which was the location of one of the field hospitals Washington set up away from the main camp at Valley Forge to quarantine the sick and prevent the spread of disease among the main group of troops. Some of the first inoculations were tried at Valley Forge. Simeon probably recovered doing light duty guarding the Continental Congress, which was meeting also at Lancaster at this time.

During the spring, the American Army recovered and learned European military skills under the direction of the famous Prussian Baron von Steubon. They were ready for battle again by June.

The Battle of Monmouth

On June 18, 1778, Washington learned that the British were abandoning Philadelphia and going to New York City. He saw this as an opportunity to catch the enemy in a vulnerable position. The British soldiers carried heavy packs and the weather was very hot while marching across the sandy marshlands of New Jersey. The going was slow. Washington instructed his troops to wear light clothing and light packs and to chase the tired British down.[51]

Simeon's regiment was the second in line in the advance group put under the command of General Charles Lee.[52] On the June 28th, the advance group caught up with the

---

[51] McDowell, The Revolutionary War, page 136.

[52] Lossing, The Pictorial Field-Book, Volume 2, pages 148 to 163.

British near Monmouth Court House and started to fight. The advanced group was outnumbered and General Lee lost control of his troops, who started falling back on their own. When General Washington arrived at the head of the main force, he chastised Lee, rallied the troops, and established a battle line. What followed was the longest, bloodiest, and hottest battle of the war. Simeon's unit was on the front line. Molly Pitcher became legendary at Monmouth for bringing water to the American troops and finally firing cannon herself when most of the artillery troops were wounded. The furious battle stopped at sundown. The British used the darkness to escape to New York City. The Battle of Monmouth was the last major battle of the war in the northern colonies.

Simeon's muster cards match historical accounts of the route taken by the American army afterwards through White Plains, New York to camps in Rhode Island.

The Battle of Rhode Island

The French fleet wanted to use Aquidneck Island, Rhode Island to land French infantry reinforcements for the war. However, a British force of over 7,000 troops was already dug in on Aquidneck Island. Simeon's unit was a part of a 10,000 troop American force that included many militia units from New England.

On August 29, 1778, the Americans fiercely tried to drive the British off the island. Bad weather complicated the effort, and the objective was not obtained. The French fleet was damaged by the weather and retreated to Boston for repairs.

Simeon is shown on furlough at his home in Dartmouth, Massachusetts from September, 1778 through March, 1779. He may have been recovering from wounds he suffered at the Battle of Rhode Island.

When Simeon rejoined his unit in April, things were in a very sorry state. The soldiers had not been paid in five months, inflation had made the Continental currency worthless, they were on half rations, and George Washington was appealing to the Colonial governors for aid warning, "there is every appearance that the Army will infallibly disband in a fortnight." Captain James Jones, Simeon's company commander, resigned his commission on April 24, 1779 because of the conditions.[53] His lieutenant, Thomas Hunt, took over the company. Then a muster card dated June 15, 1779 shows Simeon as deserted. Like most other soldiers, he gave up and went home to tend to his family and his farm.

The Battle of Springfield

Despite the poor conditions, an amnesty appeal went out to soldiers to return to their units in the following spring. Simeon Fuller and many of his comrades, including Captain James Jones, decided to continue the fight and officially returned to service at Washington's camp at Morristown,

---

[53] Massachusetts Soldiers and Sailors, Volume 8, page 925.

New Jersey on April 30, 1780.[54]

Many units had to be reorganized due to casualties and deserters who did not return. Simeon was put in Captain Thomas Hunt's Company designated the 4th Company under the 9th Regiment, which was formed from a combination of the remnants of three former regiments and put under the command of Colonel Henry Jackson.

However, the deprivations continued, and the ability of Washington's 4,000 troops assembled at Morristown to support the cause of independence appeared to be very shaky. General Clinton, the commander of British forces in New York, recognized this problem and decided that a demonstration of British strength would cause American soldiers to desert in large numbers and scare civilians to give allegiance to the King, again.[55] Accordingly, he sent 5,000 British troops under General Kryphausen from Staten Island to Elizabethtown, New Jersey.

Using Elizabethtown as a base camp, the British made raids into New Jersey towns, burning homes, and killing indiscriminately. The raids had the opposite effect and increased the resolve of the Americans. The British met great resistance from local militia and civilians. Finally, on June 23, 1780, the British were stopped at the town of Springfield by Continental Army troops dispatched from

---

[54] Ibid, Volume 6, page 186 and Volume 8, page 925.

[55] Ward, Christopher, The War of the Revolution, Volume 2, (The MacMillan Company, New York, 1952), pages 620 and 621.

their camp at Morristown. The fighting was brief but furious. Simeon's unit held the Vauxhall Bridge against the right column of the British. The battle ended with the British withdrawal back to New York.[56]

The Battle of Springfield is the last engagement in which Simeon Fuller can be placed. His unit, the 16th Regiment was disbanded on January 1, 1771 at New Windsor, New York, ten miles north of West Point on the Hudson River. He was placed in the 9th Regiment of Foot which continued until January 1, 1783. His muster cards show that he was near West Point, New York from January to April, 1781. Units there guarded the Hudson River traffic and encircled New York City. George Washington considered West Point to be the most strategic point in preventing the British from dividing the colonies. Simeon's last muster card was dated May 1, 1781. The British surrendered at Yorktown the following October. No other records of Simeon Fuller's service exist after this time.

After the war, Simeon went back to Dartmouth and lived there until about 1792. At that time, he moved to a farm near the town of Wheelock in Caledonia County, Vermont. He lived there until his death on November 25, 1808.[57]

It is difficult for us today to appreciate the courage it took for patriots like Simeon Fuller to seek independence under the greatest hardships from a government they had always

---

[56] Ibid, pages 620 to 623.

[57] Will, Volume 4, 1808-19, pages 111-113, Danville, Vermont.

known. If they lost the war, it probably meant death or life in prison at hard labor. We owe much to their bravery and tenacity.

130. **Francis**[5] **Webster** (Joseph Stancel[4], Samuel[3], Thomas[2], Thomas[1]), born 20 Jul 1794 in Fisherfield, Merrimack Co., New Hampshire.[58] He married on 26 Jul 1829 in Hatley, Quebec, Canada **Nancy Whitcomb**, born about 1806 in <Hatley, Quebec, Canada>.

Children of Francis Webster and Nancy Whitcomb were as follows:

163   i   **Adelaide M.**[6] **Webster**, born about 3 Feb 1834; died 21 Jan 1852 in Barnston, Quebec, Canada. Notes: DEATH: Freewill Baptist Church records, Barston, Quebec, Canada.

164   ii   **Horatio**[6] **Webster**, born about 1840.

---

[58]   BIRTH: 1861 Census, Hatley, Quebec, Canada, p. 116.

Sixth Generation

This generation, the Third Great Grandchildren of Thomas and Sarah Webster, saw and participated in the expansion of the United States to new frontiers. They also lived through the horrors of the Civil War. These people were pioneers who settled in the wilderness, fought the Indians, and overcame many obstacles to raise their families. They saw transportation technology begin to transform their world with the introduction of the steam engine and riverboats.

143. **Baker^6 Webster** (Davison^5, Waldron^4, Joshua^3, Thomas^2, Thomas^1), born 5 Mar 1807 in Newfield, Maine; died 3 Oct 1868 in Fort Dodge, Iowa. He married **Louisana (---)**, born 15 Jun 1803 in Parsonfield, Maine; died 27 Mar 1890 in Fort Dodge, Iowa.

Children of Baker Webster and Louisana (---) were as follows:

   165   i   **Hannah^7 Webster**.

   166   ii   **Abbie Ann^7 Webster**, born 15 Dec 1834.

   167   iii   **Caroline Adelia^7 Webster**, born 2 Oct 1837; died 16 Nov 1847 in Sandown, New Hampshire.

   168   iv   **Davison^7 Webster**, born 16 May 1845 in Strafford, New Hampshire; died 1 Aug 1903 in Fort Dodge, Iowa. He married on 25 Dec 1865 in Fort Dodge, Iowa **Emma Thomas**.

+ 169   v   **Baker^7 Webster Junior**, born 11 Sep 1846 in Sandown, New Hampshire; died 15 Jan

Sixth Generation

		1923 in Fort Dodge, Iowa. He married **Hannah Scott**.
170	vi	**Benjamin**[7] **Webster**, born 26 Sep 1848.
171	vii	**Francis Mariah**[7] **Webster**, born 1850 in Sandown, New Hampshire; died 26 Oct 1857 in Manona, Iowa.
172	viii	**John**[7] **Webster**, born 1851 in Manona, Iowa; died 17 Dec 1932 in Guthrie, Oklahoma.

158. **John H.**[6] **Webster** (Samuel[5], Joseph Stancel[4], Samuel[3], Thomas[2], Thomas[1]), born 4 Feb 1814 in New York; died 15 Mar 1876 in Green Twp., Iowa Co., Iowa, at the age of 62, and was buried in Bethel Cemetery, Johnson County, Iowa..[59] He married on 26 May 1836 in Sandusky Co., Ohio **Mary Magdalene Moomey**, born 29 Jul 1816 in Circleville, Pickaway Co., Ohio; died 19 Mar 1902 in Greene Twp., Iowa Co., Iowa, daughter of Jacob Moomey and Mary Magdalene Bruner at the age of 85, and was buried in Bethel Cemetery, Washington Township, Johnson County, Iowa.[60]

John was an identical twin. Birth record source is entry in an account book which his twin brother David maintained.

---

[59] DEATH! John died of Typhoid fever at his home in Iowa. The middle initial "H" is seen in an 1840 census of Sandusky County, Ohio.

[60] MARRIAGE: May 26, 1836 in Sandusky County, Ohio from early records at the Hayes Memorial Library at Fremont, Ohio. In 1850, she and her family lived in Pleasant Township, Seneca County, Ohio, next to her brother John and her parents.

Sixth Generation

The account book also showed the birth dates of his children.

John and Mary Webster moved from Ohio to Iowa in 1851. Their last three children were born in Iowa. Heading the party coming from Ohio to Iowa were Jacob Moomey and his wife Mary Magdelene (Bruner) Moomey.

Jacob Moomey was a veteran of the War of 1812 and received bounty land in Iowa for that service. This grant of bounty land was the motivation for the move of a large extended family.

Besides his son-in-law, John Webster, and daughter, Mary Magdelene, Jacob's daughter, Christina, and her husband, George Wiseman, also came. In addition, Jacob Moomey's sons, John, Jacob, and Peter, and their families came to Iowa in this large family group.
John and Mary Webster purchased a farm for $150 in Green Township, Iowa County, Iowa and lived good lives there.

As for John Webster's later life in Iowa, some insights are obtained from a letter written to me by Howard Webster, dated November 4, 1989:

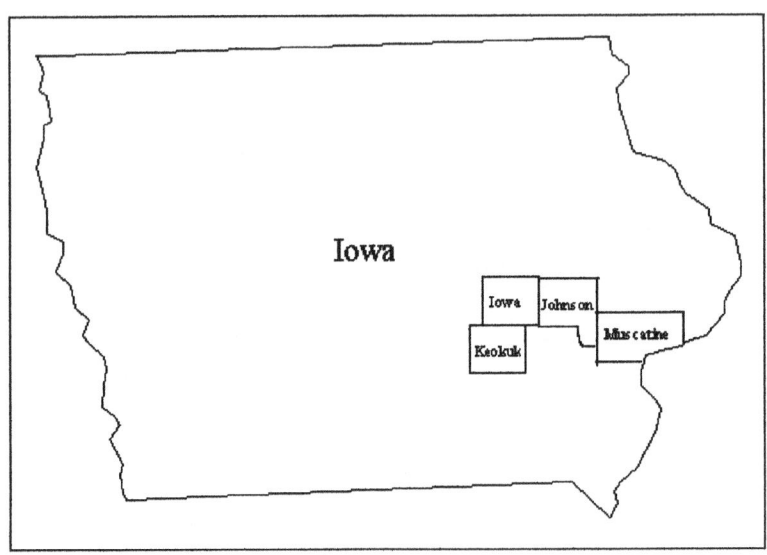

Figure 4 – Map of Iowa showing relevant points.

"I lived until I was 18 on the old Webster homestead where Great Grandfather John and Mary Webster settled after moving from Ohio. The farm is still in the family. My brother, Wayne, owns it today. No one lives on the place, because the old house got into such bad condition the cost of restoration would have been very great so we felt we would have to tear it down. We hated to see it go because of all the memories associated with it. There was a large and beautiful grove of native hardwood trees surrounding the Webster home and much of this grove of trees was still there when I was living there."

"Grandfather Freling and his brother, John, lived with us, so I grew up hearing them tell of their own boyhoods and all the happenings in the family. Freling and John were around ten years old when the Civil War started. Their brother Daniel was in the war and several other cousins. Freling and John said they were most unhappy that they could not go off to war."

"Great Grandfather was a licensed preacher in the United Brethren Church and as long as he was living he would conduct services for the family and others who cared to come. In the summer, services were in the grove of trees. When his daughter, Harriett, got married, the ceremony was also in the grove."

"Great Grandfather also started a brick factory and a drain tile factory as well as a saw mill near his home on the banks of Old Mans Creek, a smallish river or large creek. They first built a log and earth dam on the creek and ran the mill with water power but later secured a steam engine. He made the bricks used to build his home and also sawed the lumber for it."

"My Grandfather, Freling, and his brother, John, lived on in the old home with their mother after the death of John in 1872, and for a while their brother, Lafayette, helped operate the brick factory, but, in later years, Lafayette moved to Long Beach, California, and a Mr. Hiram Frank became a partner in the brick factory. Mr. Frank was a bachelor and lived with the Webster family. About 1909, they sold the factory and all the equipment, and the new owner only operated it for about two years when the steam engine blew up setting fire to the wooden buildings housing the machinery, the drying shed, etc., and all was destroyed by this fire. Today, one can tell where the kiln was because

Sixth Generation

of the numerous brick fragments in the ground."

Figure 5 – John and Mary Webster (Circa 1860). Children of John H. Webster and Mary Magdalene

Sixth Generation

Moomey were as follows:
- + 173   i   **Simeon M.**[7] **Webster**, born 13 Mar 1837 in Sandusky, Erie Co., Ohio; died 24 Dec 1865 in Woodbine, Johnson Co., Iowa. He married **Eliza Hannah Yoakam**.
- + 174   ii   **Harriet**[7] **Webster**, born 7 Sep 1838 in Sandusky Co., Ohio; died 20 Nov 1916. She married **Virgil Fry**.
- + 175   iii   **William Daniel**[7] **Webster**, born 16 Aug 1840 in Seneca Co., Ohio; died 6 Apr 1927 in Gypsum, Saline Co., Kansas. He married (1) **Laura Augustine**; (2) **Nancy Jane Jester**.
- + 176   iv   **M. Lafayette**[7] **Webster**, born 1 Sep 1842 in Seneca Co., Ohio; died about 1923 in California. He married **Mary Ann Armstrong**.
-     177   v   **Malinda**[7] **Webster**, born 7 Apr 1845 in Seneca Co., Ohio; died 26 Nov 1862 in Iowa. Died of typhoid fever at age 17.
-     178   vi   **Jacob**[7] **Webster**, born 15 Feb 1847 in Seneca Co., Ohio; died 8 Oct 1847 in Seneca Co., Ohio.
- + 179   vii   **Nancy**[7] **Webster**, born 21 Jun 1849 in Seneca Co., Ohio; died 29 Jan 1918 in Windham, Iowa. She married **Abraham Lewis**.
- + 180   viii   **Frehling Sylvester**[7] **Webster**, born 19 Dec 1851 in Iowa City, Johnson Co., Iowa; died 24 Jan 1929 in Greene Twp., Iowa Co., Iowa. He married **Florence Rowena**

Sixth Generation

Anderson.

181 ix **John Charles[7] Webster**, born 17 Mar 1856 in Iowa Co., Iowa; died 27 May 1925 at the age of 69, and was buried 28 May 1925 in Oakland Cemetery, Iowa City, Johnson County, Iowa.. He was never married and was crippled by rheumatic fever as a young man. He lived all his life with his brother Frehling.

182 x **Emma Josephine[7] Webster**, born 15 Jun 1859 in Iowa Co., Iowa; died of typhoid fever at four years old 15 May 1864 in Iowa.

Figure 6 – John Webster's Brick Factory (Circa 1870)

Sixth Generation

Figure 7 – The children of John and Mary Webster. Standing left to right: Harriet, John Charles, and Nancy. Seated left to right: William Daniel, M. Lafayette, and Frehling Sylvester.
(Circa 1870)

Sixth Generation

Mary Magdalene (Moomey) Webster's Ancestry

The Moomey (Moomy or Mummy) family was German speaking and among the many German immigrants to come into Maryland and Pennsylvania in the late 1700s. Mary Magdalene (Moomey) Webster's father, Jacob Moomey was born about 1789 in Lancaster County, Pennsylvania and her mother, Mary Magdalene Bruner was born in Maryland, 16 March 1793. They were married at the town of Lancaster, Fairfield County, Ohio, 15 June 1811.[61] Jacob had an uneventful enlistment in the War of 1812 where he marched up into Quebec but was not involved in any engagements.

The 1820 census indicates they were in adjoining Pickaway County, Ohio, in Washington Township which is near Circleville. By 1830, they were in Ballville Township in Sandusky County. In 1840 and 1850, they were living in adjoining Pleasant Township of Seneca County. This 1850 household showed Jacob age 63, Mary 61, Peter 21, Catherine 19, and also Jefferson 5 and Clarissa 3. The last two were probably grandchildren. Adjoining households were those of son John and Elizabeth, son-in-law John Webster and Mary Magdalene, son Jacob and his wife Effa, and a Mary Bruner, age 81, living with a Mary Bruner, 14.

In 1851, Jacob's family and some of his married children moved to Iowa when he was granted bounty land for his

---

[61] National Archives War of 1812 Application #26926.

Sixth Generation

War of 1812 service.[62] According to a Tama County, Iowa history biography of one of Mary's brothers, Christian Bruner (born 1799 in Pennsylvania), this was "before there was even a railroad in the state." Christian Bruner had 19 children of two wives. His biography goes on to say, "Some of the children, of course, married and remained in Ohio, but when the family started for the west in wagons, it made quite a colony in itself. A start was made in the fall of 1851; on the way the Bruners were joined by the Overmires, and the strengthened party spent the following winter in Iowa City, and in the spring of 1852 located in Tama County." John and Mary Moomey Webster had a son born December, 1851, in Iowa City, Johnson County, Iowa.

Jacob settled in Johnson County, receiving 40 acres of bounty land. In 1856, he received an additional grant of 120 acres. During this time, Jacob also operated a fanning mill, which separated grain from chaff.

In 1860, Jacob and Mary Moomey were in Union Township of Johnson County. Peter's family was in the adjoining household. Their post office was Iowa City.

About 1869, Peter's family moved to Muscatine County, where Peter had a butcher business. The 1870 Census shows Jacob and Mary, now about 80 years old, in Peter's household in Wilton Township, Wilton Junction. Jacob died in adjoining Moscow Township on September 24, 1872.

---

[62] National Archives Bounty Land Warrants: Act of 28 Sep 1850, #143821. 48,933_40_50 for 40 acres of Iowa land and Act of 3 Mar 1855; 70,668_120_55. for 120 acres of Iowa land.

Sixth Generation

About that time, Peter's family moved to Keokuk County, when the butcher business failed. Peter again took up farming as a tenant. In the 1880 Census, Mary was still living with them; her age was given as 87. It has been told that when she was about 90 or so, she went with Peter's family to visit relatives in Iowa County, about 30 miles away and a very full day's ride. She made the trip seated in a rocking chair in the wagon and was described as robust.

Family legend has it that Jacob's father, John Jacob Moomey, was a Revolutionary War soldier. The most likely candidate I could find in the National Archives was a pension application R16627 (The "R" means Rejected) submitted by a John Mummy who in 1829 was living in Circleville, Pickaway County, Ohio where Jacob and Mary were living during the 1820 Census. He says that he enlisted in the Continental Army and served in the Battle of Brandywine which we lost. He was captured by the British and imprisoned in Philadelphia. When the British left Philadelphia, he escaped, made his way back to his home in the mountains of western Maryland, got married, and never bothered to find his unit.

Mary Magdalene Bruner's father was also named Jacob. There is confusion by researchers over where Jacob Bruner was born. According to census and family records he was born about 1770. According to legend in the Martin Bruner family, he was born in Strausberg, a village east of Berlin, Germany and came here with his widowed mother about 1791-2. The same legend has it that his father had been affluent and a soap manufacturer in Strausberg. The ship

Sixth Generation

"Fair American" had on board two passengers, Jacob Bronner and Maria Dorothea Bronner, listing her first, as cabin passengers, landing in Sept., 1791 at Philadelphia. Legend has it that the mother brought her son to America to save him from conscription in the Prussian Army at the start of the Napoleonic Wars. The family was believed to have been Jewish.

There was also a Jacob Bronner born in 1770 in Lancaster County, Pennsylvania to Casper Brunner and Ursula Shellenberger. There is a town called Strausberg in Lancaster County.

It is possible that Jacob Bruner married three times. The name of his first wife, Christina Sattler, is taken from the baptismal certificate of Christina Bruner Zehrung. It could have been spelled Sattler, Staller, Stadler, etc. Nothing further can be found on her. She was definitely dead by Oct., 1812 when Jacob married Margaret Ebright of Bright in Fairfield, Pickaway County, Ohio. However, according to the Martin Bruner family, Martin had no idea he was not a full brother to the other children until he was an adult. This might lead one to suspect that Christina died between 1803 (birth of Margaret) and 1807 when Martin was born and Jacob had married again. The son, Peter, was most likely by Margaret Ebright as she was in his favor and against the other children in legal documents partitioning land in Seneca County, Ohio.

159. **David**[6] **Webster** (Samuel[5], Joseph Stancel[4], Samuel[3], Thomas[2], Thomas[1]), born 4 Feb 1814 in New York; died 1

Sixth Generation

Jan 1893 in Green Twp., Iowa Co., Iowa. He married on 29 Oct 1835 in Findlay, Hancock Co., Ohio **Ann Elizabeth Teatsworth**, born about 1827 in Ohio; died before 1860.[63]

An early history of Hancock County, Ohio says that David Webster, son of Samuel, married Ann Elizabeth Teatsworth and was a blacksmith in Findley, Ohio before 1840.

He received an injury to his leg which became infected and had to be amputated. In later years, he is remembered as wearing a wooden leg. His wife said she was not going to be married to a man with one leg who could not make a living, and so she divorced him. The divorce was granted on charges of adultery in the Hancock County Court in July, 1847.

She received two pieces of property and complete custody of their daughter, Henrietta.

Consequently, he was dependent on his brothers for a place to live. The 1860 Noble County, Indiana census shows him living in the household of his brother, Simeon. He was in Iowa by the census of 1865 living in the household of his twin brother, John, and continued to live in the household until his death in about 1900. He earned his keep by repairing shoes and boots. He is buried in Bethel Cemetery beside his twin.

He is remembered as being very kind, a wonderful singer,

---

[63] BIRTH! 1850 Noble Co., IN census, p. 203. MARRIAGE! "History of Hancock County"

Sixth Generation

and a great story teller.

The Webster family records of births and deaths in these early generations were in the back of a ledger book that had the primary function of recording business transactions. The transactions in the book are from his shoe and boot repair business. Therefore, David was the keeper of the family records.

Children of David Webster and Ann Elizabeth Teatsworth were as follows:
- 183   i   **Daniel W.**[7] **Webster**, born about 1841 in Indiana.[64]
- 184   ii   **Henrietta**[7] **Webster**.

160. **Simeon**[6] **Webster** (Samuel[5], Joseph Stancel[4], Samuel[3], Thomas[2], Thomas[1]), born 11 Apr 1816 in New York. He married (1) on 12 Jun 1837 in Sandusky Co., Ohio **Polly A. DePew**, born <1816> in <Sandusky Co., Ohio>; died before 1848; (2) about 1848 **Rhoda (---)**, born about 1831 in Ohio. Rhoda is found in 1900 Soundex as living in Oklahoma without Simeon.

Children of Simeon Webster and Polly A. DePew were as follows:
- 185   i   **Barbara**[7] **Webster**, born about 1839 in Ohio; died after 1861. She married on 3 Jul 1861 **Francis Trask**.

---

[64] BIRTH! 1850 and 1860 censuses.

Sixth Generation

+ 186   ii   **John David**[7] **Webster**, born about 1841 in Ohio; died 1872 in Noble Co., Indiana. He married **Susanah Deck**.
187   iii   **Laurel**[7] **Webster**, born about 1843 in Ohio; died after 1864. She married on 28 Apr 1864 **Jacob Sparrow**.

Children of Simeon Webster and Rhoda (---) were as follows:
188   i   **Sarah E.**[7] **Webster**,, born about 1849 in Indiana.
189   ii   **Mary**[7] **Webster**, born about 1853 in Illinois.
190   iii   **Samuel**[7] **Webster**, born about 1856 in Indiana.
191   iv   **Richard**[7] **Webster**, born about 1859 in Indiana. Probably died about 1860.
192   v   **Amina**[7] **Webster**, born about 1863 in Indiana.
193   vi   **Richard**[7] **Webster**, born about 1861 in Indiana.
194   vii   **Alvoretta**[7] **Webster**, born about 1867 in Indiana.

161. **Nancy O.**[6] **Webster** (Samuel[5], Joseph Stancel[4], Samuel[3], Thomas[2], Thomas[1]), born 14 Feb 1826 in Kentucky; died 1888 in Washington Co., Kansas. She married (1) in Ohio **Elihu Lindsey**, born about 1821 in <Kentucky>; died 1853 in Ottawa Co., Ohio; (2) **Lyman Green**, born <1822> in <Kentucky> after the Civil War.

Sixth Generation

They moved to Iowa for a short time and then moved on to Washington County, Kansas.

Children of Nancy O. Webster and Elihu Lindsey were as follows:
195 i **Elihu⁷ Lindsey Jr.**, born in Ottawa Co., Ohio.
196 ii **William⁷ Lindsey**, born about 1848 in Ottawa Co., Ohio; died 1868.

Figure 8 – Lyman Green and Nancy O. Webster
(Circa 1870)

Seventh Generation

The Fourth Great Grandchildren of Thomas and Sarah Webster lived in the last half of the 1800s and the first part of the 1900s. They were pioneers who settled the nation's frontiers. They were drawn mostly by the prospect of owning their own farm. They helped tame the West and saw the expansion of the United States to the Pacific Ocean. The railroads were built during their lives and revolutionized travel and commerce for them. They saw the horse drawn carriage replaced by the automobile.

169. **Baker**[7] **Webster Junior** (Baker[6], Davison[5], Waldron[4], Joshua[3], Thomas[2], Thomas[1]), born 11 Sep 1846 in Sandown, New Hampshire; died 15 Jan 1923 in Fort Dodge, Iowa. He married on 1 Nov 1872 in Fort Dodge, Iowa **Hannah Scott**, born 6 Aug 1850 in Ohio; died 28 Apr 1905 in Fort Dodge, Iowa, daughter of Robert Scott and Mary (---).

Children of Baker Webster Junior and Hannah Scott were as follows:

- 197   i   **Nellie**[8] **Webster**, born 9 May 1872 in Fort Dodge, Iowa. She married on 26 Jun 1894 in Fort Dodge, Iowa **Joseph Wonders**.
- 198   ii   **Fannie**[8] **Webster**, born 8 Nov 1878; died in West Virginia. She married **Cassius Blackstone**.
- 199   iii   **Abbie**[8] **Webster**, born 15 Jul 1880; died in Indianapolis, Indiana. She married on 31 Aug 1904 in Fort Dodge, Iowa **Roy**

Seventh Generation

		Brieghtol.
200	iv	**Charles G.**[8] **Webster**, born 30 Jun 1882 in Fort Dodge, Iowa; died 21 Mar 1958. He married on 8 Jul 1910 in Fort Dodge, Iowa **Mary K. Yost**.

173. **Simeon M.**[7] **Webster** (John H.[6], Samuel[5], Joseph Stancel[4], Samuel[3], Thomas[2], Thomas[1]), born 13 Mar 1837 in Sandusky, Erie Co., Ohio; died of typhoid fever on 24 Dec 1865 in Woodbine, Johnson Co., Iowa, at the age of 28. He married on 10 Jul 1858 in Woodbine, Johnson Co., Iowa **Eliza Hannah Yoakam**, born 31 Jul 1839 in Marion Co., Ohio; died 21 Apr 1921 at the age of 81 in Woodbine, Johnson Co., Iowa, daughter of Joseph Yoakam and Nancy Higgins. Simeon and Eliza were buried in Bethel Cemetery, Johnson County, Iowa.

Children of Simeon M. Webster and Eliza Hannah Yoakam were as follows:

201	i	**Mary E.**[8] **Webster**, born 6 Apr 1860. She married **John R. Tupper**.
202	ii	**Laurence**[8] **Webster**, born 1862; died 15 Oct 1864 at two years old.
203	iii	**Joseph Norman**[8] **Webster**, born 12 May 1865; buried in Woodbine, Iowa. He married **Cora T. Scull** and lived to be 90 years old.

174. **Harriet**[7] **Webster** (John H.[6], Samuel[5], Joseph

Stancel⁴, Samuel³, Thomas², Thomas¹), born 7 Sep 1838 in Sandusky Co., Ohio; died 20 Nov 1916 at the age of 78. She married **Virgil Fry**, born in 1834 in Sandusky Co., Ohio.

Children of Harriet Webster and Virgil Fry were as follows:

- 204 i **Charles Sylvester⁸ Fry**, born Aug 1859; died 1 Nov 1913 at the age of 54.
- 205 ii **Frank L.⁸ Fry**, born Nov 1860.
- 206 iii **Kate O.⁸ Fry**, born Feb 1862. She married **A. E. Main**.
- 207 iv **Mary Jane⁸ Fry**, born Sep 1864. She married **(---) Garrett**.

175. **William Daniel⁷ Webster** (John H.⁶, Samuel⁵, Joseph Stancel⁴, Samuel³, Thomas², Thomas¹), born 16 Aug 1840 in Seneca Co., Ohio; died 6 Apr 1927 in Gypsum, Saline Co., Kansas at the age of 86.⁶⁵ He married (1) in 1860 in Iowa **Laura Augustine**, born <1839> in <Iowa>; died 1873 in Iowa City, Iowa; (2) on 3 Jan 1874 at the age of 34 in Iowa City, Johnson Co., Iowa **Nancy Jane Jester**, born 12 May 1853 in Mt. Pleasant, Henry Co., Iowa; died 20 Apr 1931 at the age of 78 in Canton, McPherson Co., Kansas, daughter of John Charles "Jesse" Jester and Elizabeth

---

⁶⁵ BIRTH: Civil War pension records obtained at the National Archives. Birth dates of the children were obtained from the 1910 U.S. Census (Kansas, Marion County, Lehigh Township, Sheet 8B).

Seventh Generation

Amanda White.[66] Nancy also married (1) Reuben Augustine, brother of Laura, 1870 in Washington, Iowa. He was born 1849 in Mt. Pleasant, Henry County, Iowa. Reuben died Sep 1872 in Talleyrand, Iowa, at the age of 23.

Children of William Daniel Webster and Laura Augustine were as follows:

   208   i   **Charles Eugene[8] Webster**, born 27 Apr 1861; died 12 Sep 1882 in Family Farm, Roxbury, Kansas. Died due to a kick in the head by a horse and is buried on the farm in a field beside the Lindsberg-Roxbury Road.

+ 209   ii   **William Wesley[8] Webster**, born 7 Mar 1863 in Indian County, Iowa; died 25 Oct 1933. He married **Wilemina Johanna "Minnie" Cludas**.

+ 210   iii   **Almyra May[8] Webster**, born 8 Sep 1865. She married **William Manuels**.

+ 211   iv   **John Ellsworth[8] Webster**, born 6 Apr 1869; died 21 Mar 1941. He married **Maggie Gable**.

   212   v   **Florence[8] Webster**, born 8 Oct 1871.

Children of William Daniel Webster and Nancy Jane Jester were as follows:

---

[66] Nancy's birth, marriage,_ and death information were obtained from William Daniel Webster's Civil War pension records from the National Archives and Kansas death certificate #59 3632.

Seventh Generation

+ 213 i Marion Jonas[8] Webster, born 21 Dec 1874 in Iowa; died 21 Oct 1932. He married **Lida Lee**.
  214 ii Electra Ann[8] Webster, born 1 May 1876 in Iowa; died 16 Sep 1878 in Iowa.
+ 215 iii Mary Etta[8] Webster, born 16 Mar 1877 in Iowa; died in California. She married **Carl Giddings**.
+ 216 iv Virgil Franklin[8] Webster, born 31 Jan 1879 in near Lindsburg, McPherson Co., Kansas; died 25 Jul 1962 in Canton, McPherson Co., Kansas. He married **Pearl H. Whittenberg**.
+ 217 v Howard Lincoln[8] Webster, born 16 Oct 1881 in near Lindsburg, McPherson Co., Kansas; died 27 Nov 1969 in El Dorado, Butler Co., Kansas. He married **Elizabeth "Bessy" Wining**.
+ 218 vi Daniel Clay[8] Webster, born 12 Dec 1883 in Crazy Ridge, McPherson County, Kansas; died 24 Feb 1992 in Roxbury, Kansas at age 108. He married **Lillian Keefer**.
+ 219 vii Ella Maude[8] Webster, born 4 Jul 1885 in Kansas; died 14 May 1949. She married **Revillow Royce**.
  220 viii Maggie Malinda[8] Webster, born 19 Jun 1887 in Kansas; died 22 Sep 1920. She married **Arthur Dole**, born <1883> in <Kansas>.
+ 221 ix Benjamin Harrison[8] Webster, born 15 Jun

Seventh Generation

			1889 in Lindsberg, McPherson Co., Kansas; died 2 Feb 1964 in Great Bend, Barton Co., Kansas. He married **Laveta Fern Oldfield**.
+	222	x	**Lawrence Lester**[8] **Webster**, born 9 Sep 1891 in Canton, McPherson Co., Kansas; died 16 May 1954 in El Dorado, Butler Co., Kansas. He married **Nora Ollenberger**.
+	223	xi	**Bertha Jane**[8] **Webster**, born 22 Oct 1893 in Durham, Kansas; died 11 Jan 1971 in Marion Co., Kansas. She married **John F. Unruh**.
+	224	xii	**Minnie Alvina**[8] **Webster**, born 12 Jun 1894 in Kansas. She married **Alban Swallander**.
+	225	xiii	**Ruth Lorena**[8] **Webster**, born 12 Jan 1897 in Kansas; died 25 Jun 1930. She married **Herman Hackler**.
+	226	xiv	**Lee McKinley**[8] **Webster**, born 5 May 1899 in Kansas; died 9 Feb 1984 in Valley Center, Sedgwick Co., Kansas. He married **Waneta Fullenwiter**.

William Daniel Webster was known as "Dan." He is one of the most interesting characters in our line. Dan was six feet tall, light complexion, dark eyes, brown hair, and his occupation was farmer. This physical description is contained in his Civil War pension records.

William Daniel Webster served in the Civil War as a Private in Company K, 44th Regiment, Iowa Infantry from June 1 to September 15, 1864. He enlisted in Davenport,

Seventh Generation

Iowa and was taken to Tennessee probably from Davenport to Memphis by riverboat on the Mississippi River. One document in his pension records said he was deployed near La Grange, Tennessee, which was 30 miles east of Memphis and in Confederate territory.

The Battle of Shiloh had occurred just east of La Grange on April 6 and 7, 1862. The Union forces under General Ulysses S. Grant were taken by surprise by Confederates under General Albert S. Johnson. The Union forces suffered more losses than the Confederates but managed to hold the area, which was known thereafter as the "Hornet's Nest." In 1863, the area was a supply point supporting the siege of Vicksburg, Mississippi farther down river. In 1864, the southwestern Tennessee area was still hotly contested. The famous cavalry Confederate General Nathan Bedford Forrest was raiding the Union forces there under General William Tecumseh Sherman, who was using the area as a staging base for his drive into the deep South where he would burn Atlanta.

Southwestern Tennessee is close to the Mississippi River flood plain and at that time was full of swamps and all the unhealthy conditions that go with that type of terrain. For his pension, William Daniel Webster testified that he was at or near La Grange, Tennessee on September 8, 1864 and came down with malaria followed by typhoid fever. Shortly after he was taken sick, he was granted a leave of absence and was returned home and discharged at Davenport, Iowa on September 15, 1864. He was nursed back to health by his first wife, Laura, but suffered from loss of hearing and poor health for the rest of his life

Seventh Generation

because of those diseases.

In the Public Broadcasting System series on the Civil War aired in September, 1990, it said half of all Iowa men of military age served in the Civil War filling 46 regiments in all. A total of 13,001 died: 3,540 in combat, 515 while prisoners of war, and 8,498 of disease. Those figures were typical. When viewed in this context, William Daniel Webster's experience is more understandable.

William Daniel had five children by his first wife, Laura. After she died in 1873, he married Nancy Jane (Jester) Augustine, the widow of Reuben Augustine, Laura's brother. Nancy had one child from her first marriage. Dan and Nancy had another 14 children of their own. Sixteen of their twenty total children were alive when Dan applied for his Civil War pension in 1898. He listed them on the back of the legal sized sheet as required. They filled it up. Dan wrote on the bottom of the list, "Please send a little more paper next time."

Dan and Nancy and their family left Iowa for Kansas about October, 1878. They traveled in covered wagon and arrived in Kansas in time to build a dugout along the Smokey Hill about ten miles northwest of Roxbury before his son, Virgil Franklin Webster, was born on January 31, 1879.

They homesteaded a farm six miles west of Roxbury in 1880. The farm was located in the northeast corner of the section south of the Roxbury-Lindsberg road and west of the Galva road. The family lived in a dugout until a house was built in the spring of 1882 in the southeast corner of the

160 acre plot. About 1888, the family moved to the West Kentucky district about three miles east of Johnstown.

Around 1896, the family moved to a farm near Durham. It was while they were living here that William Daniel lost his left arm. He was riding in a wagon and happened to rest his arm on the end of a shotgun. The shotgun went off accidentally and shattered his arm. He was taken on home and his son, Daniel Clay, aged fourteen, was sent for the doctor. Daniel Clay, who was ill at the time, had to ride bareback on a horse in freezing weather 13 miles to Canton and back. William's arm had to be cut off at the shoulder. Do not feel too sorry for Daniel Clay; he lived to be 108 years old.

They moved to a farm at Dole's Park near Canton and on to Lehigh in 1905. They then moved to a farm north of Canton in 1912 and then to one near Waldick. In 1919, Dan and Nancy bought a house in Canton and lived there until Dan died on April 6, 1927 at the age of 87. Nancy died on April 20, 1931 when she was 78.

Aunt Elaine says that Dan and Nancy had over one hundred grandchildren, and that, in their final years at family gatherings, Dan would gather his grandchildren around him and entertain them with stories including some from his past. One such story tells of an Indian squaw stopping by his boyhood home in Seneca County, Ohio to talk to his mother, Mary. The squaw put her baby wrapped in a papoose style back carrier outside the door and went in. A boar gored the baby to death. The squaw buried her child, said something over its grave, and went away.

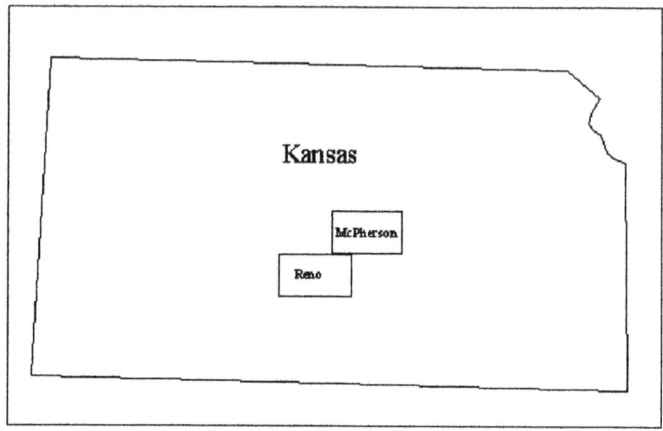

Figure 9 – Map of Kansas showing relevant points.

Aunt Elaine also said that her Grandfather claimed to have some Indian blood, but I have not found any truth to that piece of family lore. It was probably just some of Dan's creative yarn spinning.

Another interesting story concerns Florence Webster, Dan's fifth child by his first wife, Laura. Florence went on the stage. Actors were held in low esteem at the time, and Dan disowned his daughter for sinking so low. Years later she wrote her brother, John, that she would be coming through the Canton Railroad Station and would like to see him. Even though John was married at this time and was living in a home of his own, he did not dare go against his father's wishes and go see his sister. She was never heard of again.

Seventh Generation

Nancy Jane (Jester) Augustine Webster's Ancestry

Nancy Jane's parents were John Charles "Jesse" and Elizabeth Amanda (White) Jester. They show up very clearly on page 72 of the 1860 Census in Washington County, Iowa. Jesse was a carpenter. He was born in Ohio as was his wife, Elizabeth, and their firstborn child, Amanda. Nancy Jane is shown accurately as a six year old female born in Iowa. From the records of the children's births, it is evident that they came to Iowa from Ohio between 1847 and 1852.

However, an examination of Jesters in Ohio does not clearly show this family. Perhaps they were in a larger household there. Most of the Jesters were concentrated in the southwestern quadrant of Ohio. Their 1850 Census records show many of the older Jester family members were born in Delaware.

Delaware is noted for being settled in large measure by Swedish people in Colonial times. The 1800 Census shows many Jesters in Delaware. Surnames with the "ster" suffix like Jester and Webster are Teutonic and Scandinavian in origin. Therefore, although this is only conjecture, it seems likely that our Jesters were Swedish people who first settled in Delaware and then moved west.

Record of movements:
    Left Iowa for Kansas about October, 1878. Traveled in covered wagon and arrived in Kansas in time to build a dugout along the Smokey Hill about ten miles northwest of

Seventh Generation

Roxbury before his son, Virgil Franklin Webster, was born on January 31, 1879.

Homesteaded a farm six miles west of Roxbury in 1880. The farm was located in the northeast corner of the section south of the Roxbury-Lindsberg road and west of the Galva road. The family lived in a dugout until a house was built in the spring of 1882 in the southeast corner of the 160 acre plot.

About 1888, the family moved to the West Kentucky district about three miles east of Johnstown.

Around 1896, the family moved to a farm near Durham. It was while they were living here that William Daniel lost his arm. He was riding in a wagon and happened to rest his arm on the end of a shotgun. The shotgun went off accidentally and shattered his arm. He was taken on home and Dan, aged fourteen, was sent for the doctor. Dan, who was ill at the time, had to ride bareback on a horse in freezing weather 13 miles to Canton and back. William's arm had to be cut off.

Moved to a farm at Dole's Park near Canton and on to Lehigh in 1905.

They then moved to a farm north of Canton in 1912 and then to one near Waldick. In 1919, William Daniel and Nancy bought a house in Canton and lived there until William died on April 6, 1927 at the age of 87. Nancy died on April 20,1931 when she was 78.

There was family talk about having gone to Oklahoma to look over land that was in the Cherokee Strip. Wild Bill Hickock was along for part of the trip.

Seventh Generation

Figure 10 – William Daniel and Nancy Jane Webster and their children.

Seated left to right: William Daniel, Lee McKinley, Ruth Lorena, and Nancy Jane. Standing front left to right: Maggie, Jonas Marion, Ella Maude, Daniel Clay, Bertha Jane, Minnie Alvina, and Mary Etta. Standing in back from left to right: Howard Lincoln, Benjamin Harrison, Lawrence Lester, and Virgil Franklin.
(Circa 1910)

Seventh Generation

Also, our Great grandfather (William Daniel Webster) was offered a quarter section of land that is now part of the southern part of the old business district in Hutchinson in trade for his team and wagon. Apparently this was either when they went to look over land on the Strip or another trip when they were looking for land.

176. **M. Lafayette**[7] **Webster** (John H.[6], Samuel[5], Joseph Stancel[4], Samuel[3], Thomas[2], Thomas[1]), born 1 Sep 1842 in Seneca Co., Ohio; died about 1923 in California. He married **Mary Ann Armstrong**, born 1846 in Seneca Co., Ohio.

Children of M. Lafayette Webster and Mary Ann Armstrong were as follows:

- 227 i **Francis Ellen**[8] **Webster**, born 4 Oct 1863; died 9 Mar 1951. She married **Clarence Anderson**.
- 228 ii **Minnie Moselle**[8] **Webster**, born 12 Mar 1869; died 23 Mar 1942. She married **John C. Cross**.
- 229 iii **Jennie Orilla**[8] **Webster**, born 1871; died May 1872.
- 230 iv **Laura May**[8] **Webster**, born 18 Oct 1874; died 23 Jan 1965. She married **Fred H. Crow**.
- 231 v **Charles Sylvester**[8] **Webster**, born 2 Mar 1876; died after 1972. He married **Jennie Mae Patterson**.
- 232 vi **Clayton Emery**[8] **Webster**, born Oct 1878;

Seventh Generation

died 7 May 1889.
233   vii   **Josephine Maude**[8] **Webster**, born 15 Oct 1880; died after 1972. She married **Elmer E. Yoder**.
234   viii   **Wesley Blaine**[8] **Webster**, born 15 Aug 1884. He married **Emma Durian**.

179. **Nancy**[7] **Webster** (John H.[6], Samuel[5], Joseph Stancel[4], Samuel[3], Thomas[2], Thomas[1]), born 21 Jun 1849 in Seneca Co., Ohio; died 29 Jan 1918 in Windham, Iowa, at the age of 68. She married **Abraham Lewis**, born 1845 in Seneca Co., Ohio.

Children of Nancy Webster and Abraham Lewis were as follows:
235   i   **Frank**[8] **Lewis**.

180. **Frehling Sylvester**[7] **Webster** (John H.[6], Samuel[5], Joseph Stancel[4], Samuel[3], Thomas[2], Thomas[1]), born 19 Dec 1851 in Iowa City, Johnson Co., Iowa; died 24 Jan 1929 in Greene Twp., Iowa Co., Iowa at the age of 77, and was buried in Oakland Cemetery, Iowa City, Johnson County, Iowa. He married in 1883 in Johnson County, Iowa **Florence Rowena Anderson**, born 1855 in Iowa City, Johnson Co., Iowa.

Frehling continued with the Webster family business of brick and tile factory and saw mill.

Seventh Generation

Children of Frehling Sylvester Webster and Florence Rowena Anderson were as follows:

   236   i   **Ethel May**[8] **Webster**, born 26 Oct 1884; died 29 Apr 1932. She married **Daniel E. Yoder**.

   237   ii   **Elmer Earl**[8] **Webster**, born 6 Sep 1886. He married **Mamie Mae Cox**.

+ 238   iii **Arthur H.**[8] **Webster**, born 8 Jan 1888 in Iowa County, Iowa; died 29 Apr 1939 in Iowa City, Iowa. He married **Blanche Bernice Buck**.

Figure 11 – Frehling and Florence Webster and children. Seated left to right: Frehling, Ethel May, and Florence. Standing left to right: Elmer Earl and Arthur H. (Circa 1900)

- - - - - - - - - - -

Seventh Generation

186. **John David**[7] **Webster** (Simeon[6], Samuel[5], Joseph Stancel[4], Samuel[3], Thomas[2], Thomas[1]), born about 1841 in Ohio; died 1872 in Noble Co., Indiana, and was buried in Wright Cemetery, York Township, Noble County, Indiana. He married **Susanah Deck**.

Children of John David Webster and Susanah Deck were as follows:
- 239 i **George**[8] **Webster**.
- 240 ii **Ira**[8] **Webster**.

John David Webster was in the Civil War in Company B, 12th Ohio Cavalry. He was a dispatcher for Sheridan's Raiders. His horse was shot out from under him and smashed his leg. He was taken prisoner by the Confederates and put in either Andersonville or Libby prison. He was released at the end of the war, but, due to the poor conditions he suffered under while in prison, his leg never fully healed and finally killed him in 1872.

Eighth Generation

The members of the eighth generation of Thomas and Sarah Webster's family were their fifth great grandchildren. They lived at the turn of the century and into the twentieth century. During this period, they experienced the Industrial Revolution and saw their lives transformed by modern innovations, such as the automobile, the airplane, indoor plumbing, the electric light, and motion pictures. They also saw America participate in two world wars of unprecedented scale and fury. They suffered the Great Depression of the 1930s as well.

209. **William Wesley^8 Webster** (William Daniel^7, John H.^{6}, Samuel^5, Joseph Stancel^4, Samuel^3, Thomas^2, Thomas^1), born 7 Mar 1863 in Indian County, Iowa; died 25 Oct 1933. He married **Wilemina Johanna "Minnie" Cludas.**

William Wesley Webster was a blacksmith in Canton, Kansas most of his life.

Children of William Wesley Webster and Wilemina Johanna "Minnie" Cludas were as follows:
- 241 i **Howard^9 Webster.**
- + 242 ii **Stanley Ross^9 Webster**, born 8 Jun 1886 in Ness County, Kansas; died 5 Feb 1960. He married **Mabel A. Spurrier.**

210. **Almyra May^8 Webster** (William Daniel^7, John H.^{6}, Samuel^5, Joseph Stancel^4, Samuel^3, Thomas^2, Thomas^1),

Eighth Generation

born 8 Sep 1865. She married **William Manuels**.

Children of Almyra May Webster and William Manuels were as follows:
  243   i   **Pearl^9 Manuels**.
  244   ii   **William^9 Manuels**.
  245   iii **Edith^9 Manuels**.

211. **John Ellsworth^8 Webster** (William Daniel^7, John H.^{6}, Samuel^5, Joseph Stancel^4, Samuel^3, Thomas^2, Thomas^1), born 6 Apr 1869; died 21 Mar 1941. He married **Maggie Gable**.

Children of John Ellsworth Webster and Maggie Gable were as follows:
  246   i   **Arthur^9 Webster**.
  247   ii   **Gertrude^9 Webster**.
  248   iii **John Raymond^9 Webster**.

213. **Marion Jonas^8 Webster** (William Daniel^7, John H.^{6}, Samuel^5, Joseph Stancel^4, Samuel^3, Thomas^2, Thomas^1), born 21 Dec 1874 in Iowa; died 21 Oct 1932. He married **Lida Lee**, born 1878 in Iowa.

Children of Marion Jonas Webster and Lida Lee were as follows:
  249   i   **Marrium^9 Webster**.

Eighth Generation

215. **Mary Etta⁸ Webster** (William Daniel⁷, John H.⁶, Samuel⁵, Joseph Stancel⁴, Samuel³, Thomas², Thomas¹), born 16 Mar 1877 in Iowa; died in California. She married **Carl Giddings**, born 1873 in Iowa.

Children of Mary Etta Webster and Carl Giddings were as follows:
- 250 i **Chester⁹ Giddings**.
- 251 ii **Edna⁹ Giddings**.
- 252 iii **Mildred⁹ Giddings**.
- 253 iv **Marion⁹ Giddings**.
- 254 v **Clarice⁹ Giddings**.

216. **Virgil Franklin⁸ Webster** (William Daniel⁷, John H.⁶, Samuel⁵, Joseph Stancel⁴, Samuel³, Thomas², Thomas¹), born 31 Jan 1879 in near Lindsburg, McPherson Co., Kansas; died 25 Jul 1962 in Canton, McPherson Co., Kansas. He married on 1 Mar 1905 in Canton, McPherson Co., Kansas **Pearl H. Whittenberg**, born <1883> in <Kansas>.

Children of Virgil Franklin Webster and Pearl H. Whittenberg were as follows:
- 255 i **Milton⁹ Webster**.
- 256 ii **Violet⁹ Webster**.
- 257 iii **Laverne⁹ Webster**.
- 258 iv **Kenneth⁹ Webster**.

Eighth Generation

259 v Lucille^9 Webster.
260 vi Dorothy^9 Webster.

217. **Howard Lincoln^8 Webster** (William Daniel^7, John H.^{6}, Samuel^5, Joseph Stancel^4, Samuel^3, Thomas^2, Thomas^1), born 16 Oct 1881 in near Lindsburg, McPherson Co., Kansas; died 27 Nov 1969 in El Dorado, Butler Co., Kansas. He married on 27 Apr 1906 in El Dorado, Butler Co., Kansas **Elizabeth "Bessy" Wining**, born 19 Oct 1887 in Carbon Cliff, Rock Island Co., Illinois. She was the daughter of William Shippen Wining and Mary Anna Fuller. Elizabeth died 29 Oct 1942 in Winfield, Cowley County, Kansas, at the age of 55, and was buried in Canton Cemetery, McPherson County, Kansas.

Children of Howard Lincoln Webster and Elizabeth "Bessy" Wining were as follows:

+ 261 i **Gerald^9 Webster**, born 13 Oct 1907 in Canton, Kansas; died 6 Apr 1990 in Canton, Kansas. He married **June Fuller**.
+ 262 ii **William Wining^9 Webster**, born 19 Mar 1910 in Canton, Kansas. He married **Kathryn Holiday**.
   263 iii **Madlyn E.^{9} Webster**, born 10 Jun 1912; died 7 Aug 1914.
   264 iv **M. Marjorie^9 Webster**, born 26 Mar 1915 in Canton, McPherson County, Kansas. She married on 9 Sep 1930 **Paul Cox**.

Eighth Generation

+ 265 v **Maxine D.**[9] **Webster**, born 17 Nov 1917 in Gypsum, McPherson County, Kansas. She married **Gene Cagle**.
+ 266 vi **Pauline**[9] **Webster**, born 1 Sep 1920 in Midian, Butler County, Kansas. She married **N. A. Johnston**.
+ 267 vii **Norma Geraldine**[9] **Webster**, born 28 May 1927 in Midian, Butler County, Kansas. She married **Edwin R. King**.

218. **Daniel Clay**[8] **Webster** (William Daniel[7], John H.[6], Samuel[5], Joseph Stancel[4], Samuel[3], Thomas[2], Thomas[1]), born 12 Dec 1883 in Crazy Ridge, McPherson County, Kansas; died 24 Feb 1992 in Roxbury, Kansas at 108 years old. He married on 8 Nov 1913 **Lillian Keefer**, born 29 Jul 1891 in Admire, Kansas; died 5 Aug 1965 in Lindsberg, Kansas, daughter of John Grant Keefer and Alice Baxter.

Children of Daniel Clay Webster and Lillian Keefer were as follows:

+ 268 i **Everett Winston**[9] **Webster**, born 28 Dec 1914. He married (1) **Elizabeth (---)**; (2) **Gretel Nahr**; (3) **Cacilia Mayer**.
+ 269 ii **Wendell Sherwood**[9] **Webster**, born 27 Mar 1916. He married **Dorothy Karley**.
+ 270 iii **Wilma Allene**[9] **Webster**, born 5 Dec 1918. She married **George Hurch**.
+ 271 iv **Warren Frances**[9] **Webster**, born 20 Mar 1923 in Roxbury, Kansas. He married

Eighth Generation

+ 272	v	Margaret Spongberg. **Ronald Daniel**^{9} **Webster**, born 14 Nov 1925. He married **Ruth Fite**.
+ 273	vi	**Alice Jane**^{9} **Webster**, born 4 Feb 1928. She married **Darrell Carlson**.
+ 274	vii	**Patricia Lillian**^{9} **Webster**, born 24 Mar 1931; died 6 Nov 1979. She married **Marvin Johnson**.

219. **Ella Maude**^{8} **Webster** (William Daniel^7, John H.^{6}, Samuel^5, Joseph Stancel^4, Samuel^3, Thomas^2, Thomas^1), born 4 Jul 1885 in Kansas; died 14 May 1949. She married **Revillow Royce**, born <1881> in <Kansas>.

Children of Ella Maude Webster and Revillow Royce were as follows:

275	i	**Harold**^{9} **Royce**.
276	ii	**Marcellas**^{9} **Royce**.

221. **Benjamin Harrison**^{8} **Webster** (William Daniel^7, John H.^{6}, Samuel^5, Joseph Stancel^4, Samuel^3, Thomas^2, Thomas^1), born 15 Jun 1889 in Lindsberg, McPherson Co., Kansas; died 2 Feb 1964 in Great Bend, Barton Co., Kansas. He married on 16 May 1911 in Hutchinson, Reno Co., Kansas **Laveta Fern Oldfield**, born 8 Aug 1890 in Canton, McPherson Co., Kansas; died 6 Mar 1971 in Lyons, Rice Co., Kansas, daughter of Alonzo David

Eighth Generation

Oldfield and Clara Myrtes Kirby.[67]

Benjamin Harrison was born on a farm near Lindsborg June 15, 1889. "Harry", as he was popularly known, spent many years of his life in the Roxbury, Gypsum, and Lindsborg communities.

At one time, he owned and operated a Ford dealership in Canton at the location now occupied by Friendly Chevrolet. For about ten years, he was in the automobile business in Lyons.

He retired as an automobile dealer and salesman and died Sunday, February 2, 1964, at St. Rose Hospital, Great Bend. He had been in failing health for about a year.

Harry and Laveta were married May 16, 1911 by a Justice of the Peace, J. M. Jordan, in the town of Hutchinson, Reno County, Kansas, not their home county of McPherson, and only about four months before the birth of their first child, my father.[68] Despite this unfortunate beginning, they had a successful lifelong marriage.

Children of Benjamin Harrison Webster and Laveta Fern Oldfield were as follows:
+ 277 i **Reginald Dale**[9] **Webster**, born 26 Aug

---

[67] DEATH: Kansas Death Certificate #71 004793.

[68] MARRIAGE: Source is "Reno County Kansas Early Marriage Records," 1872-1913, The Reno County Genealogical Society, 1982, Mennonite Press, Inc., page 264.

Eighth Generation

			1911 in Canton, McPherson Co., Kansas; died 2 Jul 1965 in Wichita, Sedgwick Co., Kansas at age 53. He married **Julia Berg**.
+	278	ii	**Elaine Maxine**[9] **Webster**, born 24 Feb 1914 in Canton, McPherson Co., Kansas; died 22 Jul 2008 in Parkersbury, West Virginia at age 94. She married **Dore Verl Wilson**.
+	279	iii	**Virginia Enola**[9] **Webster**, born 6 Aug 1916 in McPherson, McPherson Co., Kansas; died 5 Jul 1976 in Lyons, Rice Co., Kansas. She married **Noel Johnson Knight**.
	280	iv	**Inez Ruth**[9] **Webster**, born 9 Sep 1918 in Canton, McPherson Co., Kansas; died 28 Nov 2004 in Lyons, Kansas. She married (1) in 1937 in Alma, Nebraska **Ralph Watson**, born 14 Aug 1909 in Haven, Kansas; died 1972 in Lyons, Kansas; (2) on 14 Aug 1974 in Abilene, Kansas **Noah Eugene Rider**, born 25 Sep 1924 in Salina, Kansas.
+	281	v	**Randall Harry**[9] **Webster**, born 31 Mar 1923 in Canton, McPherson Co., Kansas; died 15 Jun 1994 in Parkersburg, Wood Co., West Virginia. He married **Peggy Houser**.
+	282	vi	**Bob Rex Alvin**[9] **Webster**, born 29 Oct 1925 in Canton, McPherson Co., Kansas. He married **Ruth Riffel**.

Eighth Generation

222. **Lawrence Lester**[8] **Webster** (William Daniel[7], John H.[6], Samuel[5], Joseph Stancel[4], Samuel[3], Thomas[2], Thomas[1]), born 9 Sep 1891 in Canton, McPherson Co., Kansas; died 16 May 1954 in El Dorado, Butler Co., Kansas.[69] He married **Nora Ollenberger**, born <1895> in <Canton, McPherson Co., Kansas>.

Children of Lawrence Lester Webster and Nora Ollenberger were as follows:
283 i **Earl**[9] **Webster**.
284 ii **Emerson**[9] **Webster**.
285 iii **Evelyn**[9] **Webster**.
286 iv **Velma**[9] **Webster**.
287 v **Lester**[9] **Webster**.

223. **Bertha Jane**[8] **Webster** (William Daniel[7], John H.[6], Samuel[5], Joseph Stancel[4], Samuel[3], Thomas[2], Thomas[1]), born 22 Oct 1893 in Durham, Kansas; died 11 Jan 1971 in Marion Co., Kansas. She married **John F. Unruh**, born 12 Apr 1891 in Marion Co., Kansas; died 4 Jun 1974 in Marion Co., Kansas, son of John J. Unruh and Mary Friesen.

Children of Bertha Jane Webster and John F. Unruh were as follows:
+ 288 i **Elman J.**[9] **Unruh**, born 31 Jan 1917 in

---

[69] BIRTH and DEATH: Funeral program, The Danielson-Ball Chapel.

Eighth Generation

		Marion Co., Kansas. He married (1) Lvonne Linke; (2) **Melvia Layrie Dillon**.
+ 289	ii	**Clarice Elsie**^{9} **Unruh**, born 28 Apr 1918 in Marion Co., Kansas. She married **Norman Ludwig Haefner**.
+ 290	iii	**Louis Daniel**^{9} **Unruh**, born 24 Jul 1919 in Marion Co., Kansas. He married (1) **Frankie Harper**; (2) **Reatric Mick**.
291	iv	**Harold Marvin**^{9} **Unruh**, born 27 Nov 1922 in Marion Co., Kansas. He married on 21 Nov 1945 **Nelva Ruth Hoch**.
+ 292	v	**Erma Mae**^{9} **Unruh**, born 12 Sep 1928 in Marion Co., Kansas. She married **William C. Holley**.
+ 293	vi	**Doris Jane**^{9} **Unruh**, born 18 Aug 1932 in Marion Co., Kansas. She married **Donald Lee Farmer**.
+ 294	vii	**Jonas Boyd**^{9} **Unruh**, born 28 Apr 1934 in Hillsboro, Marion Co., Kansas. He married **Francess Lorraine Klassen**.

224. **Minnie Alvina**^{8} **Webster** (William Daniel^7, John H.^{6}, Samuel^5, Joseph Stancel^4, Samuel^3, Thomas^2, Thomas^1), born 12 Jun 1894 in Kansas. She married **Alban Swallander**, born 1890 in Kansas.

Children of Minnie Alvina Webster and Alban Swallander were as follows:

295	i	**Delores Lamar**^{9} **Swallander**.

Eighth Generation

225. **Ruth Lorena**[8] **Webster** (William Daniel[7], John H.[6], Samuel[5], Joseph Stancel[4], Samuel[3], Thomas[2], Thomas[1]), born 12 Jan 1897 in Kansas; died 25 Jun 1930. She married **Herman Hackler**, born 1893 in Kansas.

Children of Ruth Lorena Webster and Herman Hackler were as follows:
   296   i   **Nona Mae**[9] **Hackler**.

226. **Lee McKinley**[8] **Webster** (William Daniel[7], John H.[6], Samuel[5], Joseph Stancel[4], Samuel[3], Thomas[2], Thomas[1]), born 5 May 1899 in Kansas; died 9 Feb 1984 in Valley Center, Sedgwick Co., Kansas. He married **Waneta Fullenwiter**, born 1903 in Kansas.

Children of Lee McKinley Webster and Waneta Fullenwiter were as follows:
   297   i   **William**[9] **Webster**.
   298   ii   **Robert**[9] **Webster**.

238. **Arthur H.**[8] **Webster** (Frehling Sylvester[7], John H.[6], Samuel[5], Joseph Stancel[4], Samuel[3], Thomas[2], Thomas[1]), born 8 Jan 1888 in Iowa County, Iowa; died 29 Apr 1939 in Iowa City, Iowa. He married on 14 Sep 1911 in Johnson County, Iowa **Blanche Bernice Buck**, born 19 Nov 1891 in Johnson County, Iowa; died 19 Jan 1965 in Iowa City, Iowa.

Eighth Generation

Children of Arthur H. Webster and Blanche Bernice Buck were as follows:

+ 299 i **Howard Emerson^9 Webster**, born 20 Nov 1913 in Iowa County, Iowa; died 21 Jul 1991 in Iowa City, Iowa. He married **Bernice Elizabeth Denney**.

Howard Webster and his wife Bernice were avid genealogy researchers. They laid the groundwork for this genealogy.

Ninth Generation

The ninth generation consists of the Sixth Great Grandchildren of Thomas and Sarah Webster. They lived mainly in the first half of the twentieth century. Many of them came off the farms to live in the towns and cities and to work in the factories. They suffered through the financial problems of the Great Depression. They participated in the industrialization of the workforce and in two world wars and the Korean War as well. They saw air travel become common and witnessed our first steps into space and the landing on the moon.

242. **Stanley Ross**[9] **Webster** (William Wesley[8], William Daniel[7], John H.[6], Samuel[5], Joseph Stancel[4], Samuel[3], Thomas[2], Thomas[1]), born 8 Jun 1886 in Ness County, Kansas; died 5 Feb 1960. He married on 26 Jun 1907 **Mabel A. Spurrier**, born 1 Aug 1879 in Kent, Taylor County, Iowa; died 28 Jan 1959 in Glendale, Los Angeles County, California, daughter of Samuel Franklin Spurrier and Margaret Eleanor Wickham.

Children of Stanley Ross Webster and Mabel A. Spurrier were as follows:

300 i **Stanton Frank**[10] **Webster**, born 12 Jun 1908 in McPherson, McPherson County, Kansas; died 1909 in McPherson, McPherson County, Kansas.

301 ii **Loraine Eleanor**[10] **Webster**, born 12 Jul 1908 in McPherson, McPherson County, Kansas.

Ninth Generation

+ 302　iii　**William Eugene**[10] **Webster**, born 28 Feb 1911 in Canton, McPherson County, Kansas; died 12 May 1969 in Barstow, San Bernardino County, California. He married **Lelah Bernice Nicholson**.

303　iv　**James**[10] **Webster**, born 13 Aug 1916 in McPherson County, Kansas; died 5 Jan 1997 in San Bernardino, California. He married on 27 Feb 1941 **Geraldine Griffith**.

304　v　**Geraldine Marilyn**[10] **Webster**, born 21 Oct 1918 in Kansas; died 15 May 1964.

261. **Gerald**[9] **Webster** (Howard Lincoln[8], William Daniel[7], John H.[6], Samuel[5], Joseph Stancel[4], Samuel[3], Thomas[2], Thomas[1]), born 13 Oct 1907 in Canton, Kansas; died 6 Apr 1990 in Canton, Kansas. He married **June Fuller**.

Children of Gerald Webster and June Fuller were as follows:

305　i　**Forrest**[10] **Webster**.
306　ii　**Enos**[10] **Webster**.
307　iii　**Larry**[10] **Webster**.
308　iv　**Gloria**[10] **Webster**. She married (---) **Stubbs**.
309　v　**Phyllis**[10] **Webster**. She married **Metcalf-Carner**.
310　vi　**Selma**[10] **Webster**. She married (---) **Brickle**.

Ninth Generation

311 vii Lota[10] Webster. She married (---) Miller.
312 viii Mary[10] Webster. She married (---) Gruver.

262. **William Wining**[9] **Webster** (Howard Lincoln[8], William Daniel[7], John H.[6], Samuel[5], Joseph Stancel[4], Samuel[3], Thomas[2], Thomas[1]), born 19 Mar 1910 in Canton, Kansas. He married **Kathryn Holiday**.

Children of William Wining Webster and Kathryn Holiday were as follows:
313 i **Billy**[10] **Webster**, born 3 Oct.
314 ii **Thomas**[10] **Webster**, born 28 May.

265. **Maxine D.**[9] **Webster** (Howard Lincoln[8], William Daniel[7], John H.[6], Samuel[5], Joseph Stancel[4], Samuel[3], Thomas[2], Thomas[1]), born 17 Nov 1917 in Gypsum, McPherson County, Kansas. She married **Gene Cagle**.

Children of Maxine D. Webster and Gene Cagle were as follows:
315 i **Mickey**[10] **Cagle**, born 30 Nov 1940.
316 ii **Rexter Vernon**[10] **Cagle**, born 14 Feb 1942.

266. **Pauline**[9] **Webster** (Howard Lincoln[8], William Daniel[7], John H.[6], Samuel[5], Joseph Stancel[4], Samuel[3], Thomas[2],

Thomas¹), born 1 Sep 1920 in Midian, Butler County, Kansas. She married **N. A. Johnston**.

Children of Pauline Webster and N. A. Johnston were as follows:
317   i   **Robert Stanton**^{10} **Johnston**, born 6 Oct.

267. **Norma Geraldine**^{9} **Webster** (Howard Lincoln^8, William Daniel^7, John H.^{6}, Samuel^5, Joseph Stancel^4, Samuel^3, Thomas^2, Thomas^1), born 28 May 1927 in Midian, Butler County, Kansas. She married in 1942 **Edwin R. King**.

Children of Norma Geraldine Webster and Edwin R. King were as follows:
318   i   **Edwin**^{10} **King**, born 29 Oct.
319   ii **Ernest**^{10} **King**, born 29 Oct.

268. **Everett Winston**^{9} **Webster** (Daniel Clay^8, William Daniel^7, John H.^{6}, Samuel^5, Joseph Stancel^4, Samuel^3, Thomas^2, Thomas^1), born 28 Dec 1914. He married (1) on 13 Apr 1949 **Elizabeth (---)**; (2) on 11 Feb 1960 **Gretel Nahr**, died Jul 1967; (3) on 7 Mar 1968 **Cacilia Mayer**, born 28 Jan 1934.

Children of Everett Winston Webster and Elizabeth (---) were as follows:
320   i   **Edward Daniel**^{10} **Webster**, born 19 Dec

Ninth Generation

1949. He married on 10 Aug 1974 **Ann Bernardo**.

269. **Wendell Sherwood**[9] **Webster** (Daniel Clay[8], William Daniel[7], John H.[6], Samuel[5], Joseph Stancel[4], Samuel[3], Thomas[2], Thomas[1]), born 27 Mar 1916. He married on 18 Jun 1942 **Dorothy Karley**, born 22 Feb 1920.

Children of Wendell Sherwood Webster and Dorothy Karley were as follows:
+ 321 i **Barbara Kay**[10] **Webster**, born 11 Jul 1944. She married **Ronald Porter**.
   322 ii **Wendy Karleen**[10] **Webster**, born 22 May 1949. She married on 26 Jul 1970 **Randy Hurst**, born 3 May 1945.

270. **Wilma Allene**[9] **Webster** (Daniel Clay[8], William Daniel[7], John H.[6], Samuel[5], Joseph Stancel[4], Samuel[3], Thomas[2], Thomas[1]), born 5 Dec 1918. She married on 11 Oct 1934 **George Hurch**, born 14 Dec 1905; died 11 May 1967.

Children of Wilma Allene Webster and George Hurch were as follows:
+ 323 i **Gerald Gene**[10] **Hurch**, born 16 Aug 1936. He married **Mary Anderson**.
+ 324 ii **Charles Wesley**[10] **Hurch**, born 10 Apr 1938. He married **Carolyn Hallock**.

Ninth Generation

+ 325   iii   **Robert Douglas**[10] **Hurch**, born 19 Nov 1942. He married **Mildred George**.
+ 326   iv   **Gilbert Leslie**[10] **Hurch**, born 12 Oct 1944. He married (1) **Sandra Allen**; (2) **Judy Schaaf**.
+ 327   v   **Timothy Allen**[10] **Hurch**, born 24 Jul 1948. He married **Janet Waldschmidt**.
    328   vi   **Georgia Dawn**[10] **Hurch**, born 23 Apr 1950. She married on 17 Oct 1971 **Donald Merriman**, born 19 May 1948.
+ 329   vii   **Avereil Janis**[10] **Hurch**, born 4 Mar 1955. She married **Charles Boyer**.
    330   viii   **Billie Joy**[10] **Hurch**, born 29 Aug 1956. She married on 5 Aug 1973 **Harold Peterson**, born 6 Oct 1955.

271. **Warren Frances**[9] **Webster** (Daniel Clay[8], William Daniel[7], John H.[6], Samuel[5], Joseph Stancel[4], Samuel[3], Thomas[2], Thomas[1]), born 20 Mar 1923 in Roxbury, Kansas. He married on 24 Jan 1947 **Margaret Spongberg**, born 21 May 1926.

Children of Warren Frances Webster and Margaret Spongberg were as follows:
    331   i   **Sandra Sue**[10] **Webster**, born 17 Mar 1949. She married on 11 Nov 1970 **Robert Kelly**, born 9 Mar 1949.
+ 332   ii   **Larry Wayne**[10] **Webster**, born 29 Jun 1951. He married **Barbara Sands**.

Ninth Generation

333   iii   **Denise Ann**[10] **Webster**, born 12 Mar 1955. She married on 16 Feb 1974 **Mark Lysell**, born 17 Sep 1950.

334   iv   **Gary Dean**[10] **Webster**, born 16 Mar 1957; died 3 Nov 1974.

335   v   **Jerry Lee**[10] **Webster**, born 1 Oct 1963.

272. **Ronald Daniel**[9] **Webster** (Daniel Clay[8], William Daniel[7], John H.[6], Samuel[5], Joseph Stancel[4], Samuel[3], Thomas[2], Thomas[1]), born 14 Nov 1925. He married on 21 Aug 1946 **Ruth Fite**, born 6 Sep 1929.

Children of Ronald Daniel Webster and Ruth Fite were as follows:

+ 336   i   **Katherine Ann**[10] **Webster**, born 14 Sep 1947. She married **William Wellborn**.

337   ii   **Daniel Keith**[10] **Webster**, born 24 Nov 1953.

273. **Alice Jane**[9] **Webster** (Daniel Clay[8], William Daniel[7], John H.[6], Samuel[5], Joseph Stancel[4], Samuel[3], Thomas[2], Thomas[1]), born 4 Feb 1928. She married on 1 May 1949 **Darrell Carlson**, born 21 Aug 1921.

Children of Alice Jane Webster and Darrell Carlson were as follows:

338   i   **Alice Lorraine**[10] **Carlson**, born 19 Nov 1950. She married on 19 Dec 1972

Ninth Generation

Howard Webb.
339 ii **Curtiss Darrell**[10] **Carlson**, born 6 Oct 1954; died 21 Dec 1969.

274. **Patricia Lillian**[9] **Webster** (Daniel Clay[8], William Daniel[7], John H.[6], Samuel[5], Joseph Stancel[4], Samuel[3], Thomas[2], Thomas[1]), born 24 Mar 1931; died 6 Nov 1979. She married on 26 Dec 1951 **Marvin Johnson**, born 11 Sep 1931.

Children of Patricia Lillian Webster and Marvin Johnson were as follows:
    340 i   **Paul Ryan**[10] **Johnson**, born 29 Sep 1952.
    341 ii   **Teresa Lynn**[10] **Johnson**, born 22 May 1954; died 27 May 1954.
    342 iii   **Greg Brian**[10] **Johnson**, born 6 May 1955.

277. **Reginald Dale**[9] **Webster** (Benjamin Harrison[8], William Daniel[7], John H.[6], Samuel[5], Joseph Stancel[4], Samuel[3], Thomas[2], Thomas[1]), born 26 Aug 1911 in Canton, McPherson Co., Kansas; died 2 Jul 1965 in Wichita, Sedgwick Co., Kansas.[70] He married on 2 Oct 1941 in Wichita, Sedgwick Co., Kansas **Julia Berg**, born 14 Oct 1907 in Hillsboro, Marion Co., Kansas; died 13 Mar 1982 in Wichita, Sedgwick Co., Kansas, daughter of Peter Paul

---

[70] BIRTH: Kansas birth certificate.

Ninth Generation

Berg and Juliana Schroeder.[71]

Obituary published in The Wichita Eagle on July 3, 1965:

"Reginald Webster Succumbs at 53"

Reginald D. Webster, 53, of 3015 E. Waterman, died Friday.

He was born in Canton, Kansas, and came to Wichita 25 years ago from Hillsboro, Kansas.

OCCUPATION: He was a tool and die maker for the Boeing Co. the past 20 years. (During World War II, he made B-17 and B-29 bombers.) He was a member of Albert Pike Masonic Lodge, Wichita Consistory and Midian Shrine.

Julia came from Dutch Mennonites who emigrated from Russia and Poland during the 1880's settled in central Kansas. She also married (1) Herman David CORNELSEN 22 Aug 1929 in Newton, Reno County, Kansas; they divorced in 1933. He was born 8 Feb 1903 in Alne, Marion County, Kansas. Herman died 15 Jan 1952 in Wichita, Sedgwick County, Kansas, at the age of 48, and was buried 18 Jan 1952 in Peabody, Kansas. He was an accountant, Clerk of District Court in Marion County, Post Master of Hillsboro and a loyal Democrat.

Children of Reginald Dale Webster and Julia Berg were

Ninth Generation

as follows:

+ 343   i   **Dale Douglas**[10] **Webster**, born 5 Feb 1945 in Wichita, Kansas. He married **Kathleen Louise Ferguson**.

+ 344   ii   **Larry Joe**[10] **Webster**, born 17 Nov 1946 in <Wichita, Sedgwick Co., Kansas.

Reginald had 1 stepchild:

+ 157.   iii.   **Bonnie Lou CORNELSEN**, born 30 Dec 1930.

Figure 12
Reginald and Julia Webster

Ninth Generation

278. **Elaine Maxine**[9] **Webster** (Benjamin Harrison[8], William Daniel[7], John H.[6], Samuel[5], Joseph Stancel[4], Samuel[3], Thomas[2], Thomas[1]), born 24 Feb 1914 in Canton, McPherson Co., Kansas; died 22 Jul 2008 in Parkersburg, West Virginia at age 94. She married on 6 Nov 1933 in Wichita, Sedgwick Co., Kansas **Dore Verl Wilson**, born 10 Dec 1905 in Jay County, Indiana; died 16 May 1966 in Guysville, Ohio, son of William Franklin Wilson and Jessie Lefever.

Children of Elaine Maxine Webster and Dore Verl Wilson were as follows:

+ 345   i   **Rodney Dale**[10] **Wilson**, born 27 Oct 1934 in Hillsboro, Marion County, Kansas. He married **Francis Joan Gwynn**.
+ 346   ii   **Joan Dorothy**[10] **Wilson**, born 19 Oct 1937 in Odessa, Ector County, Texas. She married **Marvin Arno Petty**.
+ 347   iii   **Michael James**[10] **Wilson**, born 15 Mar 1942 in Odessa, Ector County, Texas. He married **Josephine Loraine Simcic**.
+ 348   iv   **Steven Ross**[10] **Wilson**, born 28 Jul 1947 in Parkersburg, Wood County, West Virginia. He married **Violet Louise Liotti**.

279. **Virginia Enola**[9] **Webster** (Benjamin Harrison[8], William Daniel[7], John H.[6], Samuel[5], Joseph Stancel[4], Samuel[3], Thomas[2], Thomas[1]), born 6 Aug 1916 in McPherson, McPherson Co., Kansas; died 5 Jul 1976 in

Ninth Generation

Lyons, Rice Co., Kansas. She married on 16 Jul 1933 in Wellington, Kansas **Noel Johnson Knight**, born <1912> in <McPherson, McPherson Co., Kansas>; died in Kilgore, Texas.

Children of Virginia Enola Webster and Noel Johnson Knight were as follows:
+ 349 i **Shirley Enola**^{10} **Knight**, born 5 Jul 1936 in Goessel, Kansas. She married (1) **Gene Persson**; (2) **John Richard Hopkins**.
 350 ii **Donald**^{10} **Knight**.
 351 iii **Gloria**^{10} **Knight**.

281. **Randall Harry**^{9} **Webster** (Benjamin Harrison^8, William Daniel^7, John H.^{6}, Samuel^5, Joseph Stancel^4, Samuel^3, Thomas^2, Thomas^1), born 31 Mar 1923 in Canton, McPherson Co., Kansas; died 15 Jun 1994 in Parkersburg, Wood Co., West Virginia. He married on 21 Apr 1942 in Wichita, Sedgwick Co., Kansas **Peggy Houser**, born 21 Sep 1924 in Wichita, Sedgwick Co., Kansas; died 13 Aug 1973 in New Orleans, Louisiana.

Children of Randall Harry Webster and Peggy Houser were as follows:
+ 352 i **Pamela Kay**^{10} **Webster**, born 21 Nov 1945 in Lyons, Kansas. She married **Leo Quinton Nash Jr.**
+ 353 ii **Ginny Fern**^{10} **Webster**, born 22 Jul 1947 in Amarillo, Texas. She married (1)

Ninth Generation

Joseph Jules Blanchard Sr.; (2) Robert Joseph Bonnette.

282. **Bob Rex Alvin**[9] **Webster** (Benjamin Harrison[8], William Daniel[7], John H.[6], Samuel[5], Joseph Stancel[4], Samuel[3], Thomas[2], Thomas[1]), born 29 Oct 1925 in Canton, McPherson Co., Kansas. He married on 26 Apr 1946 in Newton, Kansas **Ruth Riffel**, born 29 Mar 1929 in Wichita, Sedgwick Co., Kansas.

Bob served in the US Navy in the Pacific during World War II.

Children of Bob Rex Alvin Webster and Ruth Riffel were as follows:
354 i **Bobby**[10] **Webster**, born about 1950 in Wichita, Kansas.

288. **Elman J.**[9] **Unruh** (Bertha Jane[8] Webster, William Daniel[7], John H.[6], Samuel[5], Joseph Stancel[4], Samuel[3], Thomas[2], Thomas[1]), born 31 Jan 1917 in Marion Co., Kansas. He married (1) in Sep 1941, divorced **Lvonne Linke**; (2) on 12 Apr 1947 in Las Vegas, Nevada **Melvia Layrie Dillon**.

Children of Elman J. Unruh and Melvia Layrie Dillon were as follows:
+ 355 i **Barbara Elaine**[10] **Unruh**, born 12 Jun

Ninth Generation

                1948. She married (1) **Timothy McEvers**; (2) **Lawrence Newman**.
356   ii   **Virginia Lee**^{10} **Unruh**.

289. **Clarice Elsie**^{9} **Unruh** (Bertha Jane^8 Webster, William Daniel^7, John H.^{6}, Samuel^5, Joseph Stancel^4, Samuel^3, Thomas^2, Thomas^1), born 28 Apr 1918 in Marion Co., Kansas. She married on 23 Dec 1948 in Haven, Kansas **Norman Ludwig Haefner**.

Children of Clarice Elsie Unruh and Norman Ludwig Haefner were as follows:
+ 357   i   **Sharon Lee**^{10} **Haefner**, born 8 Feb 1950 in Herington, Kansas. She married **Steven Lowell Blazer**.
   358   ii   **Carol Lynne**^{10} **Haefner**, born 12 Apr 1954 in McPherson, Kansas. She married on 17 Mar 1973 **Gary Lynn Stucky**.

290. **Louis Daniel**^{9} **Unruh** (Bertha Jane^8 Webster, William Daniel^7, John H.^{6}, Samuel^5, Joseph Stancel^4, Samuel^3, Thomas^2, Thomas^1), born 24 Jul 1919 in Marion Co., Kansas. He married (1), divorced **Frankie Harper**; (2) in Dec 1964 **Reatric Mick**.

Children of Louis Daniel Unruh and Reatric Mick were as follows:
   359   i   **Steve Louis**^{10} **Unruh**, born 5 Nov 1965.

Ninth Generation

292. **Erma Mae**[9] **Unruh** (Bertha Jane[8] Webster, William Daniel[7], John H.[6], Samuel[5], Joseph Stancel[4], Samuel[3], Thomas[2], Thomas[1]), born 12 Sep 1928 in Marion Co., Kansas. She married on 16 Mar 1958 in Wichita, Kansas, divorced **William C. Holley**.

Children of Erma Mae Unruh and William C. Holley were as follows:
- 360 i **Jennie Geneva**[10] **Holley**, born 9 May 1959 in Florida.
- 361 ii **Eugene Quentin**[10] **Holley**, born 26 Apr 1960 in McPherson, Kansas.
- 362 iii **Ann Marie**[10] **Holley**, born 7 Jun 1963 in Lincoln, Nebraska.

293. **Doris Jane**[9] **Unruh** (Bertha Jane[8] Webster, William Daniel[7], John H.[6], Samuel[5], Joseph Stancel[4], Samuel[3], Thomas[2], Thomas[1]), born 18 Aug 1932 in Marion Co., Kansas. She married on 22 Jun 1957 in McPherson, Kansas **Donald Lee Farmer**.

Children of Doris Jane Unruh and Donald Lee Farmer were as follows:
- 363 i **David Alan**[10] **Farmer**, born 6 Apr 1958 in Wichita, Kansas.
- 364 ii **Denise Annette**[10] **Farmer**, born 21 Apr 1961 in Wichita, Kansas.
- 365 iii **Debra Ann**[10] **Farmer**, born 20 Mar 1962 in

Ninth Generation

                Colorado Springs, Colorada.
366   iv   **Deidra Alane**[10] **Farmer**, born 20 Mar 1962 in Colorado Springs, Colorada.
367   v   **Daryl Lee**[10] **Farmer**, born 18 Feb 1965 in Colorado Springs, Colorada.

294. **Jonas Boyd**[9] **Unruh** (Bertha Jane[8] Webster, William Daniel[7], John H.[6], Samuel[5], Joseph Stancel[4], Samuel[3], Thomas[2], Thomas[1]), born 28 Apr 1934 in Hillsboro, Marion Co., Kansas. He married on 11 Mar 1962 in Inman, Kansas **Francess Lorraine Klassen**.

Children of Jonas Boyd Unruh and Francess Lorraine Klassen were as follows:
368   i   **Brian J.**[10] **Unruh**, born 18 Apr 1963 in McPherson, Kansas.

299. **Howard Emerson**[9] **Webster** (Arthur H.[8], Frehling Sylvester[7], John H.[6], Samuel[5], Joseph Stancel[4], Samuel[3], Thomas[2], Thomas[1]), born 20 Nov 1913 in Iowa County, Iowa; died 21 Jul 1991 in Iowa City, Iowa. He married on 17 Apr 1948 in Ringgold County, Iowa **Bernice Elizabeth Denney**, born 20 Jun 1919 in Ringgold County, Iowa.

Howard and Bernice Webster had a passion for family history research and their work is a significant part of the genealogy book.

Ninth Generation

Children of Howard Emerson Webster and Bernice Elizabeth Denney were as follows:

369 i **Julia Christene**[10] **Webster**, born 12 Nov 1949 in Iowa City, Iowa. She married on 1 Jun 1973 in Sarasota, Florida **Glenn Thomerson**, born 19 Oct 1940 in Glasglow, Kentucky.

370 ii **David Denney**[10] **Webster**, born 9 Oct 1954 in Iowa City, Iowa. He married on 4 Aug 1996 in Ames, Iowa **Jill Charlene King**, born 1960.

Tenth Generation

The tenth generation of the descendants of Thomas and Sarah Webster is made up of their Seventh Great Grandchildren. They lived primarily in the last half of the twentieth century and into the twenty first century. They participated in the Cold War and the Vietnam War. They are mostly city dwellers and are accustomed to high technology that their third great grandparents hardly could comprehend.

302. **William Eugene**^{10} **Webster** (Stanley Ross^9, William Wesley^8, William Daniel^7, John H.^{6}, Samuel^5, Joseph Stancel^4, Samuel^3, Thomas^2, Thomas^1), born 28 Feb 1911 in Canton, McPherson County, Kansas; died 12 May 1969 in Barstow, San Bernardino County, California. He married on 20 Oct 1931 in Lyons, Rice County, Kansas **Lelah Bernice Nicholson**, born 18 Sep 1912 in Wellington, Sumner County, Kansas; died 10 Apr 1969 in Barstow, San Bernardino County, California.

Children of William Eugene Webster and Lelah Bernice Nicholson were as follows:

    371   i   **Richard Eugene**^{11} **Webster,** born 10 Dec 1932 in Hutchinson, Harvey County, Kansas. He married on 6 Dec 1952 in Glendale, Los Angeles County, California **Doris Matthews.**

+ 372   ii   **Carol Elaine**^{11} **Webster,** born 25 Jan 1944 in Los Angeles, Los Angeles County, California. She married **Larry Morris Mooney.**

Tenth Generation

321. **Barbara Kay**[10] **Webster** (Wendell Sherwood[9], Daniel Clay[8], William Daniel[7], John H.[6], Samuel[5], Joseph Stancel[4], Samuel[3], Thomas[2], Thomas[1]), born 11 Jul 1944. She married on 25 Aug 1966, divorced **Ronald Porter**.

Children of Barbara Kay Webster and Ronald Porter were as follows:
373   i   **Darin**[11] **Porter**, born 31 Jan 1967.

323. **Gerald Gene**[10] **Hurch** (Wilma Allene[9] Webster, Daniel Clay[8], William Daniel[7], John H.[6], Samuel[5], Joseph Stancel[4], Samuel[3], Thomas[2], Thomas[1]), born 16 Aug 1936. He married in Sep 1966 **Mary Anderson**, born 30 Aug 1942.

Children of Gerald Gene Hurch and Mary Anderson were as follows:
374   i   **Monty Wayne**[11] **Hurch**, born 25 Dec 1968.

324. **Charles Wesley**[10] **Hurch** (Wilma Allene[9] Webster, Daniel Clay[8], William Daniel[7], John H.[6], Samuel[5], Joseph Stancel[4], Samuel[3], Thomas[2], Thomas[1]), born 10 Apr 1938. He married on 26 Dec 1965 **Carolyn Hallock**, born 26 Nov 1943.

Children of Charles Wesley Hurch and Carolyn Hallock were as follows:

Tenth Generation

375 i   Amanda Jane[11] Hurch, born 6 Nov 1971.
376 ii   Erin Elizabeth[11] Hurch, born 28 Feb 1974.

325. **Robert Douglas**[10] **Hurch** (Wilma Allene[9] Webster, Daniel Clay[8], William Daniel[7], John H.[6], Samuel[5], Joseph Stancel[4], Samuel[3], Thomas[2], Thomas[1]), born 19 Nov 1942. He married on 12 Sep 1964 **Mildred George**, born 5 Feb 1944.

Children of Robert Douglas Hurch and Mildred George were as follows:
377 i   David Lynn[11] Hurch, born 27 Jan 1965.

326. **Gilbert Leslie**[10] **Hurch** (Wilma Allene[9] Webster, Daniel Clay[8], William Daniel[7], John H.[6], Samuel[5], Joseph Stancel[4], Samuel[3], Thomas[2], Thomas[1]), born 12 Oct 1944. He married (1) in Jul 1965, divorced **Sandra Allen**; (2) on 12 May 1971 **Judy Schaaf**, born 21 Feb 1950.

Children of Gilbert Leslie Hurch and Sandra Allen were as follows:
378 i   Gilbert Allen[11] Hurch, born 30 Mar 1966.
379 ii   June Marie[11] Hurch, born 17 Apr 1967.

Children of Gilbert Leslie Hurch and Judy Schaaf were as follows:
380 i   Daniel Otis[11] Hurch, born 31 Dec 1973.

Tenth Generation

327. **Timothy Allen**[10] **Hurch** (Wilma Allene[9] Webster, Daniel Clay[8], William Daniel[7], John H.[6], Samuel[5], Joseph Stancel[4], Samuel[3], Thomas[2], Thomas[1]), born 24 Jul 1948. He married on 8 Jul 1967 **Janet Waldschmidt**, born 31 May 1947.

Children of Timothy Allen Hurch and Janet Waldschmidt were as follows:
  381 i **Christopher John**[11] **Hurch**, born 22 Dec 1971.
  382 ii **Nicole Lynn**[11] **Hurch**, born 1 Nov 1974.

329. **Avereil Janis**[10] **Hurch** (Wilma Allene[9] Webster, Daniel Clay[8], William Daniel[7], John H.[6], Samuel[5], Joseph Stancel[4], Samuel[3], Thomas[2], Thomas[1]), born 4 Mar 1955. She married on 8 Dec 1972 **Charles Boyer**, born 24 Apr 1953.

Children of Avereil Janis Hurch and Charles Boyer were as follows:
  383 i **Richard Edward**[11] **Boyer**, born 22 Jan 1974.

332. **Larry Wayne**[10] **Webster** (Warren Frances[9], Daniel Clay[8], William Daniel[7], John H.[6], Samuel[5], Joseph Stancel[4], Samuel[3], Thomas[2], Thomas[1]), born 29 Jun 1951. He married on 12 Jan 1974 **Barbara Sands**, born 23 Jun 1955.

Tenth Generation

Children of Larry Wayne Webster and Barbara Sands were as follows:

384 i **Tonya Maria**[11] **Webster**, born 25 Sep 1974.

336. **Katherine Ann**[10] **Webster** (Ronald Daniel[9], Daniel Clay[8], William Daniel[7], John H.[6], Samuel[5], Joseph Stancel[4], Samuel[3], Thomas[2], Thomas[1]), born 14 Sep 1947. She married on 17 Apr 1970 **William Wellborn**, born 12 Aug 1946.

Children of Katherine Ann Webster and William Wellborn were as follows:

385 i **Kathryn Jennifer**[11] **Wellborn**, born 5 Aug 1974.

343. **Dale Douglas**[10] **Webster** (Reginald Dale[9], Benjamin Harrison[8], William Daniel[7], John H.[6], Samuel[5], Joseph Stancel[4], Samuel[3], Thomas[2], Thomas[1]), born 5 Feb 1945 in Wichita, Kansas. He married on 11 Jun 1966 in Wichita, Sedgwick Co., Kansas **Kathleen Louise Ferguson**, born 24 Jul 1944 in Wichita, Sedgwick Co., Kansas, daughter of Clifford Earl Ferguson and Jean Ardis Solter.

See "About the Author" at the end of the book.

Children of Dale Douglas Webster and Kathleen Louise

Tenth Generation

Ferguson were as follows:
+ 386 i Douglas Clifford[11] Webster, born 4 Mar 1969 in Carswell AFB, Fort Worth, Tarrant Co., Texas. He married (1) **Evelyn Marie Zohlen** in 1995 in San Antonio, Texas; they divorced in 1998; (2) **Anne Marie Priestap** 17 Jun 2000 in Austin, Texas.

344. **Larry Joe**[10] **Webster** (Reginald Dale[9], Benjamin Harrison[8], William Daniel[7], John H.[6], Samuel[5], Joseph Stancel[4], Samuel[3], Thomas[2], Thomas[1]), born 17 Nov 1946 in <Wichita, Sedgwick Co., Kansas>.

Children of Larry Joe Webster and (---) were as follows:
387 i **Anita Marie**[11] **Landwehr**.

345. **Rodney Dale**[10] **Wilson** (Elaine Maxine[9] Webster, Benjamin Harrison[8], William Daniel[7], John H.[6], Samuel[5], Joseph Stancel[4], Samuel[3], Thomas[2], Thomas[1]), born 27 Oct 1934 in Hillsboro, Marion County, Kansas. He married on 21 Sep 1953 in Parkersburg, Wood County, West Virginia **Francis Joan Gwynn**, born 8 Dec 1935 in Parkersburg, Wood County, West Virginia, daughter of William Frederick Gwynn and Ada Louella Snyder.

Children of Rodney Dale Wilson and Francis Joan Gwynn were as follows:
+ 388 i **Steven Michael**[11] **Wilson**, born 8 Jan 1954

Tenth Generation

		in Parkersburg, Wood County, West Virginia. He married **Ruth Eng**.
+ 389	ii	**Deborah Sue**[11] **Wilson**, born 14 Sep 1955 in Parkersburg, Wood County, West Virginia. She married **Laban Marchmont Miles II**.
+ 390	iii	**Shawn Joseph**[11] **Wilson Sr.**, born 31 Aug 1957 in Parkersburg, Wood County, West Virginia. He married **Ruby Elaine Winkler**.
391	iv	**Beth Ann**[11] **Wilson**, born 6 Nov 1963 in Nowata, Oklahoma; died 17 Aug 1988 in Pawhuska, Osage County, Oklahoma.
+ 392	v	**David Patrick**[11] **Wilson**, born 6 Nov 1965 in Nowata, Oklahoma. He married (1) **Melanie Quinton**; (2) **Ramona Danielle Scott**.
+ 393	vi	**Phillip Timothy**[11] **Wilson Sr.**, born 4 Oct 1970 in Pawhuska, Osage County, Oklahoma. He married (1) **Brenda Smith**; (2) **Brandi Jean Spencer**.

346. **Joan Dorothy**[10] **Wilson** (Elaine Maxine[9] Webster, Benjamin Harrison[8], William Daniel[7], John H.[6], Samuel[5], Joseph Stancel[4], Samuel[3], Thomas[2], Thomas[1]), born 19 Oct 1937 in Odessa, Ector County, Texas. She married on 10 Jun 1955 in Parkersburg, Wood County, West Virginia **Marvin Arno Petty**, born 15 Mar 1935 in Parkersburg, Wood County, West Virginia, son of John Rex Petty and

Tenth Generation

Henrietta Murhl Bauman.

Children of Joan Dorothy Wilson and Marvin Arno Petty were as follows:

+ 394   i   **Lucinda Jane**[11] **Petty**, born 28 Dec 1955 in Parkersburg, Wood County, West Virginia. She married **David Robert Snider.**
+ 395   ii   **Wanda Sue**[11] **Petty**, born 17 May 1957 in Parkersburg, Wood County, West Virginia. She married (1) **Karl Wayne Kirby**; (2) **James Andrew Mace Sr.**.
+ 396   iii   **Cheryl Ann**[11] **Petty**, born 20 Dec 1958 in Parkersburg, Wood County, West Virginia. She married **James Raymond Ullom.**
   397   iv   **Judith Lynn**[11] **Petty**, born 31 Jan 1960 in Parkersburg, Wood County, West Virginia; died 7 Feb 2008 in Parkersburg, Wood County, West Virginia at the age of 48. She was the primary care giver for her grandmother Elaine (Webster) Wilson. She was well known for her church and charity work. However, Judy died under mysterious circumstances. Her burned body was found in a cellar house on the family farm about ten days after her death.
   398   v   **Kelly Dianne**[11] **Petty**, born 14 May 1962 in Parkersburg, Wood County, West Virginia. She married in Parkersburg, Wood County, West Virginia, divorced **Berry John Smith**, born 30 May 1962 in Parkersburg, Wood County, West Virginia.

Tenth Generation

347. **Michael James**[10] **Wilson** (Elaine Maxine[9] Webster, Benjamin Harrison[8], William Daniel[7], John H.[6], Samuel[5], Joseph Stancel[4], Samuel[3], Thomas[2], Thomas[1]), born 15 Mar 1942 in Odessa, Ector County, Texas. He married on 29 Dec 1963 in Fairview County, West Virginia **Josephine Loraine Simcic**, born 13 Nov 1943 in Fairmont County, West Virginia.

Children of Michael James Wilson and Josephine Loraine Simcic were as follows:
+ 399 i **Cynthia Loraine**[11] **Wilson**, born 29 Mar 1965 in Amarillo, Texas. She married (---) **Huckabee**.
+ 400 ii **Michele Lynette**[11] **Wilson**, born 29 Mar 1965 in Amarillo, Texas. She married (---) **Winstead**.

348. **Steven Ross**[10] **Wilson** (Elaine Maxine[9] Webster, Benjamin Harrison[8], William Daniel[7], John H.[6], Samuel[5], Joseph Stancel[4], Samuel[3], Thomas[2], Thomas[1]), born 28 Jul 1947 in Parkersburg, Wood County, West Virginia. He married on 3 Jun 1967 in Parkersburg, Wood County, West Virginia **Violet Louise Liotti**, born 26 May 1947 in Parkersburg, Wood County, West Virginia, daughter of Charles Liotti and Mary Morell.

Children of Steven Ross Wilson and Violet Louise Liotti were as follows:

Tenth Generation

+ 401   i   **Anthony Michael**[11] **Wilson**, born 16 Jan 1972 in Parkersburg, Wood County, West Virginia. He married **Cathleen Myer McCarthy**.
+ 402   ii   **Angela Renee**[11] **Wilson**, born 4 Dec 1976 in Parkersburg, Wood County, West Virginia. She married **Luca Dru Knapp**.

349. **Shirley Enola**[10] **Knight** (Virginia Enola[9] Webster, Benjamin Harrison[8], William Daniel[7], John H.[6], Samuel[5], Joseph Stancel[4], Samuel[3], Thomas[2], Thomas[1]), born 5 Jul 1936 in Goessel, Kansas. She married (1) in 1962 in Los Angeles, California, divorced **Gene Persson**; (2) on 22 May 1970 in London, England **John Richard Hopkins**, born 27 Jan 1931 in London, England; died 23 Jun 1998 in California.

Shirley Knight had recognized acting talent in high school. She went to Hollywood, California to seek a career in motion pictures. She successfully secured roles in major movies in the 1960s, including "Sweet Bird of Youth" and "Dark at the Top of the Stairs". She went on to act on the Broadway stage and on television. She became a well-known and award winning actress.

**Figure 13 – Shirley Knight
MGM Portrait from Early 1960s**

Shirley Knight is best known as an actress. She has done extensive work in the theatre, cinema, and television. She has had numerous honours including the Tony Award, Three Emmy Awards, Two Golden awards, two academy award nominations, the Venice Film Festival Best Actress, the Jury prize at the Cannes Film Festival (for producing the film "Dutchman"), the Joseph Jefferson award, Two Drama Desk nominations, Three Golden Globe nominations, nine Emmy nominations, etc. She holds an honorary Doctor of Fine Arts degree from Lake Forrest College. She has been politically active all her adult life and works for Handgun Control Inc., the homeless, AIDS research, and abused women. In the past she worked a great deal for civil rights and for nuclear disarmament. For eighteen months she toured the country with Eve Ensler's one woman play "The Depot" directed by Joanne Woodward to help educate and organize people to deal with the nuclear threat. She is from Kansas and has helped to start a Festival in Independence for William Inge.

Each spring she returns to participate and honor a playwright. She has directed plays and has written and directed a musical film about the homeless. In 2000 she was named Kansan of the Year and was presented with a citation from the governor.

In her work as an actress she is particularly proud of the following:

THEATER

THE THREE SISTERS directed by Lee Strasberg (Broadway)
LOSING TIME (written for her by John Hopkins) (Broadway)
LANDSCAPE OF THE BODY by John Guare (Drama Desk nomination, Joseph Jefferson award) (Chicago-Broadway)
A LOVELY SUNDAY FOR CREVE COEUR (written for her by Tennessee Williams) (Off-Broadway)
KENNEDY's CHILDREN by Robert Patrick (Tony Award) (Broadway)
ECONOMIC NECESSITY (written for her by John Hopkins) (England)
ABSENT FOREVER (written for her by John Hopkins) (Cleveland-PBS)
THE CHERRY ORCHARD (directed by Lucien Pintilie)(Arena Stage)
THE GLASS MENAGERIE (directed by Emily Mann) (McCarter)
THE YOUNG MAN FROM ATLANTA (written by Horton Foote, Tony award nomination)

CINEMA

THE DARK AT THE TOP OF THE STAIRS (directed by Delbert Mann, Academy Award nomination, Golden Globe award)
SWEET BIRD OF YOUTH (directed by Richard Brooks, Academy Award nomination, Gloden Globe nomination)
PETULIA (directed by Richard Lester)

DUTCHMAN (Best Actress Venice, Critics prize Cannes, directed by Anthony Harvey)
THE GROUP (directed by Sidney Lumet)
THE RAIN PEOPLE (written for her and directed by Francis Ford Coppola)
ENDLESS LOVE (directed by Franco Zefferelli)
STUART SMALLEY (directed by Harold Ramis)
AS GOOD AS IT GETS (directed by James Brooks)
THE DEVINE SECRETS OF THE YA-YA SISTERHOOD

TELEVISION

MISS JULIE by August Strindberg (CBC)
THE COUNTRY GIRL by Clifford Odets (NBC)
THE LIE by Ingmar Bergman (CBS)
Three plays for British Television written for her by John Hopkins.
PLAYING FOR TIME by Arthur Miller (Emmy nomination)
THIRTY SOMETHING (Emmy Award, Two Emmy nominations, directed by Edward Zwick)
LAW AND ORDER (Emmy nomination)
THE McMARTIN TRIAL (Emmy award, Golden Globe award)
MAGGIE WINTERS (TV SERIES)
Miss Knight was married to the writer John Hopkins until his death in 1998.

She has two daughters, Kaitliin Hopkins and Sophie C. Hopkins. Kaitlin is an actress and Sophie a writer. She also has a stepdaughter, Dr. Justine Hopkins. Justine teaches in

London and has just published a biography about her stepgrandfather, the sculptor and painter, Michael Ayrton.

John Hopkins began writing for television in the early sixties in England: a selection of the work produced includes: -

Original television plays

"Break-up" - Granada TV - 1958
"A Woman Comes Home" - BBC - 1961
"A Chance of Thunder" - (six-part thriller serial) - BBC - 1961
"Z Cars" - (police series - 54 episodes) - BBC - 1962/1964
"Walk a Tight Circle" - BBC - 1962
"I Took My Little World Away" - ATV - 1963
"Horror of Darkness" - BBC - 1963
"Some Place of Safety" - (an opera for television) - BBC - 1964
"A Man Like Orpheus" - (a ballet for television) - BBC - 1964
"Fable" - BBC - 1964
"A Game - like - Only a Game" - BBC - 1965
"Talking to a Stranger" - (four plays for television) - BBC - 1965
"Beyond the Sunrise" - BBC - 1967
"Walk into the Dark" - BBC - 1971
"Some Distant Shadow" - Granada TV - 1971
"That Quiet Earth"- BBC - 1971
"Fathers and Families" - (six plays for television) - BBC - 1976

"A Story to Frighten the Children" - BBC - 1978
"Hiroshima" - ShowTime Cable TV - 1995

Adaptations

"The Small Back Room" - (play for television from the novel written by Nigel Balchin) - BBC - 1958
"Mine Own Executioner" - (play for television from the novel written by Nigel Balchin) - BBC - 1959
"Dancers in Mourning" - (six-part mystery serial from the novel written by Margery Allingham) - BBC - 1959
"Death of a Ghost" - (six-part mystery serial from the novel written by Margery Allingham) - BBC - 1960
"Parade's End" - (three plays for television from the novels written by Ford Madox Ford) - BBC - 1964
"The Gambler" - (two-part serial from the novel written by Feodor Dostoevsky) - BBC - 1963
"Smiley's People" - (six-part serial from the novel written by John Le Carre) - BBC - 1984
"Codename Kyril" - (four hour mini series for television from the novel written by John Trenhaile) - Thames Television - 1987

Films

"Two Left Feet " - British Lion - (shared credit) - 1963
"Thunderball" - United Artists - (shared credit) - 1965
"Virgin Soldiers" - British Lion - (shared credit) - 1967
"The Offence" - United Artists - 1972
"Murder by Decree" - Avco Embassy - 1978
"The Holcroft Covenant" - Universal - (shared credit) - 1985

Plays

"This Story of Yours" - London - (premiere) - Royal Court Theatre – 1968; Stuttgart – 1969; New Haven – 1982; Hampstead Theatre Club – 1987; Buenos Aires – 1995.
"Find Your Way Home" - London - (premiere) - Open Space – 1970; New York - (Brooks Atkinson) – 1973; Frankfurt - (Kleist Theatre) - 1995
"Economic Necessity" - Leicester - (premiere) - (Haymarket) - 1973
"Next of Kin" - London - (premiere) - (National Theatre) - 1974
"Valedictorian" - (premiere) - Williston Northampton School - 1978
"Losing Time" - New York - (premiere) - (Manhattan Theatre Club) – 1979; Hamburg - (Berlin and Vienna) - 1983
"Absent Forever" - (premiere) - Great Lakes Theatre Festival - 1987

Born in London, John Hopkins spent his early years in Wimbledon. After National Service, he went up to St Catharine's College, Cambridge to read English. After graduation he joined the BBC as a studio manager, and subsequently, as a producer. He left the BBC and went to Granada Television for two years, where he began to write; at first for television, subsequently for the cinema, and eventually, for the theatre. He has continued to work in all three dramatic media; most recently, for the theatre, "Without Father, Without Son" and "The Mary Plays" for

Tenth Generation

the cinema, "The Cleaning Lady" and "Sing Your Own Song", and for television, "Hiroshima".

Hopkins won the British Screen Writers Guild Award for his work on dramatic series two years in succession for "Z Cars" in 1962 and 1963; the British Directors Guild Award for his mini-series "Talking to a Stranger" in 1966; and in 1969, for his contribution to "Masterpiece Theatre", an Emmy Award. He was nominated for an Edgar Allan Poe Award for his screenplay "Murder by Decree" in 1978; and nominated for a Cable Ace Award in 1995 for his television movie "Hiroshima" on ShowTime Cable Television. He won the HUMANITAS PRIZE for "Hiroshima". Mr. Hopkins is one of only two writers listed in the Encyclopedia Britannica for his contribution to television.

Children of Shirley Enola Knight and Gene Persson were as follows:
403   i   **Kaitlin**[11] **Persson**, born 1 Feb 1964 in New York, New York.

Children of Shirley Enola Knight and John Richard Hopkins were as follows:
404   i   **Sophie Cybele**[11] **Hopkins**, born 26 Nov 1968 in New York, New York.

352. **Pamela Kay**[10] **Webster** (Randall Harry[9], Benjamin Harrison[8], William Daniel[7], John H.[6], Samuel[5], Joseph Stancel[4], Samuel[3], Thomas[2], Thomas[1]), born 21 Nov 1945 in Lyons, Kansas. She married on 7 Mar 1969 in New

Tenth Generation

Orleans, Louisiana **Leo Quinton Nash Jr.**, born 12 Feb 1940 in New Orleans, Louisiana; died 19 Apr 1998 in Slidel, Louisiana.

Children of Pamela Kay Webster and Leo Quinton Nash Jr. were as follows:

    405   i   **Stacey Ann**[11] **Nash**, born 2 Oct 1969 in New Orleans, Louisiana. She married on 17 Feb 1995 **Barry Gene Brack Jr.**, born 14 Nov 1970 in Millington, Tennessee.

+ 406   ii   **Leo Quinton**[11] **Nash III**, born 29 Jul 1974 in New Orleans, Louisiana. He married **Angie Lorraine Marks**.

353. **Ginny Fern**[10] **Webster** (Randall Harry[9], Benjamin Harrison[8], William Daniel[7], John H.[6], Samuel[5], Joseph Stancel[4], Samuel[3], Thomas[2], Thomas[1]), born 22 Jul 1947 in Amarillo, Texas. She married (1) on 18 Jun 1966 in New Orleans, Louisiana **Joseph Jules Blanchard Sr.**, born 28 Aug 1946 in New Orleans, Louisiana; died 29 Jul 2001 in New Orleans, Louisiana; (2) on 29 Sep 2001 in New Orleans, Louisiana **Robert Joseph Bonnette**, born 6 Feb 1962 in New Orleans, Louisiana.

Children of Ginny Fern Webster and Joseph Jules Blanchard Sr. were as follows:

+ 407   i   **Joseph Jules**[11] **Blanchard Jr.**, born 5 Jul 1967 in New Orleans, Louisiana. He married **Tammy Darlene Collins**.

Tenth Generation

408 ii Peggy¹¹ **Blanchard**, born 15 Oct 1975 in Metairie, Louisiana.

355. **Barbara Elaine**¹⁰ **Unruh** (Elman J.⁹, Bertha Jane⁸ Webster, William Daniel⁷, John H.⁶, Samuel⁵, Joseph Stancel⁴, Samuel³, Thomas², Thomas¹), born 12 Jun 1948. She married (1) in 1966, divorced **Timothy McEvers**; (2) on 11 Jul 1971 **Lawrence Newman**.

Children of Barbara Elaine Unruh and Timothy McEvers were as follows:
409 i **Melanie Shanna**¹¹ **McEvers**, born 20 Oct 1967.

Children of Barbara Elaine Unruh and Lawrence Newman were as follows:
410 i **Keith Andrew**¹¹ **Newman**, born 7 Jun 1972.
411 ii **Wendy Collete**¹¹ **Newman**, born 28 Feb 1974.

357. **Sharon Lee**¹⁰ **Haefner** (Clarice Elsie⁹ Unruh, Bertha Jane⁸ Webster, William Daniel⁷, John H.⁶, Samuel⁵, Joseph Stancel⁴, Samuel³, Thomas², Thomas¹), born 8 Feb 1950 in Herington, Kansas. She married on 29 Nov 1968 **Steven Lowell Blazer**.

Children of Sharon Lee Haefner and Steven Lowell

Tenth Generation

Blazer were as follows:
412 i **Stacey Lynne**[11] **Blazer**, born 12 Mar 1970.

Eleventh Generation

The people of the eleventh generation are the Eighth Great Grandchildren of Thomas and Sarah Webster. They are living in the computer age and are continuing to expand the family into the future.

372. **Carol Elaine**[11] **Webster** (William Eugene[10], Stanley Ross[9], William Wesley[8], William Daniel[7], John H.[6], Samuel[5], Joseph Stancel[4], Samuel[3], Thomas[2], Thomas[1]), born 25 Jan 1944 in Los Angeles, Los Angeles County, California. She married on 29 Sep 1962 in Barstow, San Bernardino County, California, divorced **Larry Morris Mooney**, born 9 Feb 1942 in Charlotte, Mecklebery County, North Carolina, son of Lee Morris Mooney and Frances Isabelle Wilson.

Children of Carol Elaine Webster and Larry Morris Mooney were as follows:

413   i   **William Lee**[12] **Mooney**, born 10 Nov 1963 in Barstow, San Bernardino County, California.

414   ii   **Christine Elaine**[12] **Mooney**, born 17 Aug 1966 in Barstow, San Bernardino County, California. She married on 15 Sep 1998 in Bremerton, Kitsap County, Washington **Bart Calvin Mahugh**.

415   iii   **Timothy Andrew**[12] **Mooney**, born 16 Nov 1969 in Barstow, San Bernardino County, California. He married (1) **Christine Erin Miesse**; (2) **Terri Louise Hartley**.

Eleventh Generation

386. **Douglas Clifford**[11] **Webster** (Dale Douglas[10], Reginald Dale[9], Benjamin Harrison[8], William Daniel[7], John H.[6], Samuel[5], Joseph Stancel[4], Samuel[3], Thomas[2], Thomas[1]), born 4 Mar 1969 in Carswell AFB, Fort Worth, Tarrant Co., Texas. He married (1) on 22 Apr 1995 in San Antonio, Texas and divorced on 30 Apr 1998 **Evelyn Marie Zohlen**, born 25 Aug 1966 in Dallas, Dallas Co., Texas, daughter of Paul James Zohlen and Patricia Ann Harrison; (2) on 17 Jun 2000 in Austin, Texas **Anne Marie Priestap**, born 23 Aug 1973 in Warren, Ohio, daughter of Terry Edward Priestap and Joan Theresa Pane.

Children of Douglas Clifford Webster and Anne Marie Priestap were as follows:
- 416　i　**Ian Havre**[12] **Webster**, born 10 Feb 2002 in Austin, Texas.
- 417　ii　**Tayte Margaux**[12] **Webster**, born 13 Jul 2005 in Austin, Travis County, Texas.

Douglas Clifford Webster was an Ohio State Champion Cross-Country runner in high school in 1983. He was also a nationally ranked mile runner in the National Junior Olympics in 1985. Doug won a full college scholarship through the Air Force Reserve Officer Training Corps and graduated from Yale University with a degree in economics in 1991. He served as an Air Force officer from 1992 to 1996 in human intelligence. He won two awards from the Central Intelligence Agency for outstanding intelligence collecting during that period. He is now a Senior Director

Eleventh Generation

for marketing for Cisco Systems.

388. **Steven Michael**[11] **Wilson** (Rodney Dale[10], Elaine Maxine[9] Webster, Benjamin Harrison[8], William Daniel[7], John H.[6], Samuel[5], Joseph Stancel[4], Samuel[3], Thomas[2], Thomas[1]), born 8 Jan 1954 in Parkersburg, Wood County, West Virginia. He married on 11 Aug 1979 in Pawhuska, Osage County, Oklahoma **Ruth Eng**, born 24 May 1953 in Chicago, Illinois, daughter of Fred Eng and Doreen Hui.

Children of Steven Michael Wilson and Ruth Eng were as follows:
- 418　i　**Joshua Michael**[12] **Wilson**, born 15 Nov 1980 in Pawhuska, Osage County, Oklahoma.
- 419　ii　**Michelle Nicole**[12] **Wilson**, born 4 Feb 1984 in Pawhuska, Osage County, Oklahoma.

389. **Deborah Sue**[11] **Wilson** (Rodney Dale[10], Elaine Maxine[9] Webster, Benjamin Harrison[8], William Daniel[7], John H.[6], Samuel[5], Joseph Stancel[4], Samuel[3], Thomas[2], Thomas[1]), born 14 Sep 1955 in Parkersburg, Wood County, West Virginia. She married on 2 Mar 1973 in Miami, Ottawa County, Oklahoma **Laban Marchmont Miles II**, born 20 Nov 1953 in Pawhuska, Osage County, Oklahoma, son of Laban Marchmont Miles I and Annetta Labadie.

Children of Deborah Sue Wilson and Laban Marchmont

Eleventh Generation

Miles II were as follows:
+ 420   i   **Angelia Dawn**[12] **Miles**, born 18 Jul 1973 in Ponka City, Oklahoma. She married **John Ellis Thomas**.
+ 421   ii   **Laban Marchmont**[12] **Miles III**, born 1 Nov 1977 in Claremore, Oklahoma. He married **Summer Ann Trent**.

390. **Shawn Joseph**[11] **Wilson Sr.** (Rodney Dale[10], Elaine Maxine[9] Webster, Benjamin Harrison[8], William Daniel[7], John H.[6], Samuel[5], Joseph Stancel[4], Samuel[3], Thomas[2], Thomas[1]), born 31 Aug 1957 in Parkersburg, Wood County, West Virginia. He married on 8 Aug 1980 in Joplin, Missouri **Ruby Elaine Winkler**, born 6 Mar 1958 in Denver, Colorado, daughter of Donald Howard Winkler and Ruby Eleanor Meade.

Children of Shawn Joseph Wilson Sr. and Ruby Elaine Winkler were as follows:
    422   i   **Shawn Joseph**[12] **Wilson Jr.**, born 1 Mar 1981 in Bartlesville, Oklahoma.
    423   ii   **Tiffani Gwynn**[12] **Wilson**, born 7 Feb 1983 in Bartlesville, Oklahoma.
    424   iii   **Koty Ditto**[12] **Wilson**, born 17 Sep 1996 in Tulsa, Oklahoma.

392. **David Patrick**[11] **Wilson** (Rodney Dale[10], Elaine Maxine[9] Webster, Benjamin Harrison[8], William Daniel[7],

Eleventh Generation

John H.[6], Samuel[5], Joseph Stancel[4], Samuel[3], Thomas[2], Thomas[1]), born 6 Nov 1965 in Nowata, Oklahoma. He married (1) **Melanie Quinton**, an Osage-Seneca Indian, daughter of Joe Quinton and Sharon (---); (2) on 20 Feb 1999 in Eureka Springs, Arkansas **Ramona Danielle Scott**, born 29 May 1970 in Pawhuska, Osage County, Oklahoma, an Osage Indian, daughter of Carol Bayhyl.

Children of David Patrick Wilson and Melanie Quinton were as follows:
425   i   **Haylee Elizabeth**[12] **Wilson**, born 16 Sep 1994 in Pawhuska, Osage County, Oklahoma.

393. **Phillip Timothy**[11] **Wilson Sr.** (Rodney Dale[10], Elaine Maxine[9] Webster, Benjamin Harrison[8], William Daniel[7], John H.[6], Samuel[5], Joseph Stancel[4], Samuel[3], Thomas[2], Thomas[1]), born 4 Oct 1970 in Pawhuska, Osage County, Oklahoma. He married (1) on 25 Aug 1988 in Pawhuska, Osage County, Oklahoma **Brenda Smith**, born 26 Oct 1969, a Seneca Indian, daughter of Don Smith and Nancy Fortny; (2) on 23 Apr 1999 in Catossa, Oklahoma **Brandi Jean Spencer**, born 1 Nov 1976 in Tulsa, Oklahoma, a Chocotaw Indian, daughter of Edward Spencer and Wanda Jean Jones.

Children of Phillip Timothy Wilson Sr. and Brenda

Eleventh Generation

Smith were as follows:
- 426 i **Phillip Timothy**[12] **Wilson Jr.**, born 24 Jan 1989 in Bartlesville, Oklahoma.
- 427 ii **Kamree Danielle**[12] **Wilson**, born 11 Nov 1992 in Bartlesville, Oklahoma.

Children of Phillip Timothy Wilson Sr. and Brandi Jean Spencer were as follows:
- 428 i **Patrick Spencer**[12] **Wilson**, born 28 Jan 1997 in Bartlesville, Oklahoma.
- 429 ii **Tyler Christian**[12] **Wilson**, born 13 May 1998 in Bartlesville, Oklahoma.
- 430 iii **Derek Ryan**[12] **Wilson**, born 1 Dec 2001 in Bartlesville, Oklahoma.

394. **Lucinda Jane**[11] **Petty** (Joan Dorothy[10] Wilson, Elaine Maxine[9] Webster, Benjamin Harrison[8], William Daniel[7], John H.[6], Samuel[5], Joseph Stancel[4], Samuel[3], Thomas[2], Thomas[1]), born 28 Dec 1955 in Parkersburg, Wood County, West Virginia. She married on 31 Aug 1974 in Parkersburg, Wood County, West Virginia **David Robert Snider**, born 26 Feb 1954 in Toledo, Lucas County, Ohio, son of Edward Wetzel Snider and Martha Jean Mullinex.

Children of Lucinda Jane Petty and David Robert Snider were as follows:
- 431 i **Jason David**[12] **Snider**, born 17 Jan 1977 in Columbus, Franklin County, Ohio. He married on 12 Aug 2000 in Columbus,

Eleventh Generation

Franklin County, Ohio **Angela Rae Hahn**.
432   ii   **Christa Diane**[12] **Snider**, born 8 Jun 1979 in Columbus, Franklin County, Ohio.

395. **Wanda Sue**[11] **Petty** (Joan Dorothy[10] Wilson, Elaine Maxine[9] Webster, Benjamin Harrison[8], William Daniel[7], John H.[6], Samuel[5], Joseph Stancel[4], Samuel[3], Thomas[2], Thomas[1]), born 17 May 1957 in Parkersburg, Wood County, West Virginia. She married (1) in 1976 in Parkersburg, Wood County, West Virginia, divorced **Karl Wayne Kirby**, born 12 Oct 1952 in Jacksonville, Florida, son of Junior Karl Kirby and Doris Jean McKibben; (2) **James Andrew Mace Sr.**.

Children of Wanda Sue Petty and Karl Wayne Kirby were as follows:
+ 433   i   **Michelle Renee**[12] **Kirby**, born 26 Aug 1976 in Parkersburg, Wood County, West Virginia. She married **Matthew James Moore**.
434   ii   **Rebecca Diane**[12] **Kirby**, born 19 Jan 1978 in Parkersburg, Wood County, West Virginia.

Children of Wanda Sue Petty and James Andrew Mace Sr. were as follows:
435   i   **James Andrew**[12] **Mace Jr.**, born 29 Sep 1992 in Marietta, Ohio.
436   ii   **Tyler Levi**[12] **Mace**, born 26 Oct 1993 in

Eleventh Generation

Parkersburg, Wood County, West Virginia.

396. **Cheryl Ann**[11] **Petty** (Joan Dorothy[10] Wilson, Elaine Maxine[9] Webster, Benjamin Harrison[8], William Daniel[7], John H.[6], Samuel[5], Joseph Stancel[4], Samuel[3], Thomas[2], Thomas[1]), born 20 Dec 1958 in Parkersburg, Wood County, West Virginia. She married on 25 Jun 1983 in Waverly, Wood County, West Virginia **James Raymond Ullom**, born 21 Sep 1958 in Salem, Columbiana County, Ohio, son of Cecil Otto Ullom and Marjorie Ann Driscoll.

Children of Cheryl Ann Petty and James Raymond Ullom were as follows:

- 437 i **Christopher Daniel**[12] **Ullom**, born 25 Apr 1985 in Parkersburg, Wood County, West Virginia; died 12 Apr 2002 in Williamstown, Wood County, West Virginia.
- 438 ii **Nathanial Ryan**[12] **Ullom**, born 18 Jun 1987 in Parkersburg, Wood County, West Virginia.
- 439 iii **Brandon James**[12] **Ullom**, born 15 Dec 1988 in Parkersburg, Wood County, West Virginia.

399. **Cynthia Loraine**[11] **Wilson** (Michael James[10], Elaine Maxine[9] Webster, Benjamin Harrison[8], William Daniel[7], John H.[6], Samuel[5], Joseph Stancel[4], Samuel[3], Thomas[2],

Eleventh Generation

Thomas[1]), born 29 Mar 1965 in Amarillo, Texas. She married (---) **Huckabee**.

Children of Cynthia Loraine Wilson and (---) Huckabee were as follows:
- 440 i **Diana L.**[12] **Wilson**, born 22 Sep 1983 in Texas City, Texas.

400. **Michele Lynette**[11] **Wilson** (Michael James[10], Elaine Maxine[9] Webster, Benjamin Harrison[8], William Daniel[7], John H.[6], Samuel[5], Joseph Stancel[4], Samuel[3], Thomas[2], Thomas[1]), born 29 Mar 1965 in Amarillo, Texas. She married (---) **Winstead**.

Children of Michele Lynette Wilson and (---) Winstead were as follows:
- 441 i **Michael Joseph Verl**[12] **Wilson**, born 29 Jan 1983 in Texas City, Texas.
- 442 ii **Christopher D.**[12] **Patlan**, born 3 Nov 1984 in Pasadena, Texas.
- 443 iii **Aaron D.**[12] **Patlan**, born 12 Mar 1986 in Texas City, Texas.

401. **Anthony Michael**[11] **Wilson** (Steven Ross[10], Elaine Maxine[9] Webster, Benjamin Harrison[8], William Daniel[7], John H.[6], Samuel[5], Joseph Stancel[4], Samuel[3], Thomas[2], Thomas[1]), born 16 Jan 1972 in Parkersburg, Wood County, West Virginia. He married on 21 Aug 1999 in Parkersburg,

Eleventh Generation

Wood County, West Virginia **Cathleen Myer McCarthy**, daughter of John McCarthy and Marlene (---).

Children of Anthony Michael Wilson and Cathleen Myer McCarthy were as follows:
    444   i   **Dylan Michael**^{12} **Wilson**, born 11 Dec 1999 in Parkersburg, Wood County, West Virginia.

402. **Angela Renee**^{11} **Wilson** (Steven Ross^{10}, Elaine Maxine^9 Webster, Benjamin Harrison^8, William Daniel^7, John H.^{6}, Samuel^5, Joseph Stancel^4, Samuel^3, Thomas^2, Thomas^1), born 4 Dec 1976 in Parkersburg, Wood County, West Virginia. She married on 25 Sep 1999 in Parkersburg, Wood County, West Virginia **Luca Dru Knapp**, born 16 May 1977 in Parkersburg, Wood County, West Virginia; died 26 Sep 2001 in Louisville, Jefferson County, Kentucky.

Children of Angela Renee Wilson and Luca Dru Knapp were as follows:
    445   i   **Sydney Renee**^{12} **Knapp**, born 15 Aug 2001 in Louisville, Jefferson County, Kentucky.

406. **Leo Quinton**^{11} **Nash III** (Pamela Kay^{10} Webster, Randall Harry^9, Benjamin Harrison^8, William Daniel^7, John H.^{6}, Samuel^5, Joseph Stancel^4, Samuel^3, Thomas^2, Thomas^1), born 29 Jul 1974 in New Orleans, Louisiana. He

Eleventh Generation

married on 14 Feb 1996, divorced **Angie Lorraine Marks**.

Children of Leo Quinton Nash III and Angie Lorraine Marks were as follows:
- 446 i   **Katie Meshail**[12] **Nash**, born 10 Sep 1995 in Slidel, Louisiana.

407. **Joseph Jules**[11] **Blanchard Jr.** (Ginny Fern[10] Webster, Randall Harry[9], Benjamin Harrison[8], William Daniel[7], John H.[6], Samuel[5], Joseph Stancel[4], Samuel[3], Thomas[2], Thomas[1]), born 5 Jul 1967 in New Orleans, Louisiana. He married on 23 Jul 1987 in New Orleans, Louisiana **Tammy Darlene Collins**, born 12 Jul 1963 in New Orleans, Louisiana.

Children of Joseph Jules Blanchard Jr. and Tammy Darlene Collins were as follows:
- 447 i   **Justin Joseph**[12] **Blanchard**, born 14 Sep 1987 in Metairie, Louisiana.
- 448 ii   **Maegan Rae**[12] **Blanchard**, born 3 Feb 1992 in Metairie, Louisiana.

Twelfth Generation

The twelfth generation of Thomas and Sarah Webster are actively extending the family in a time of bountiful prosperity. They are confronting the threats of Islamic terrorism and war in the Middle East. Science and technology are profoundly changing their lives, most notably through the computer.

420. **Angelia Dawn**[12] **Miles** (Deborah Sue[11] Wilson, Rodney Dale[10], Elaine Maxine[9] Webster, Benjamin Harrison[8], William Daniel[7], John H.[6], Samuel[5], Joseph Stancel[4], Samuel[3], Thomas[2], Thomas[1]), born 18 Jul 1973 in Ponka City, Oklahoma. She married in Las Vegas, Nevada **John Ellis Thomas**, born 4 Jul 1974 in Houston, Texas, son of James Ellis Thomas and Susan Spivey.

Children of Angelia Dawn Miles and John Ellis Thomas were as follows:
449   i   **Tanaya Cheyene**[13] **Thomas**, born 27 Jun 1997 in Bartlesville, Oklahoma.

421. **Laban Marchmont**[12] **Miles III** (Deborah Sue[11] Wilson, Rodney Dale[10], Elaine Maxine[9] Webster, Benjamin Harrison[8], William Daniel[7], John H.[6], Samuel[5], Joseph Stancel[4], Samuel[3], Thomas[2], Thomas[1]), born 1 Nov 1977 in Claremore, Oklahoma. He married in Common Law **Summer Ann Trent**, born 24 Feb 1977 in Idaho, daughter of Benny Trent and Jeanie Park.

Children of Laban Marchmont Miles III and Summer

Twelfth Generation

Ann Trent were as follows:
   450   i   **Laban Marchmont**[13] **Miles IV**, born 29 May 1997 in Oklahoma City, Oklahoma.

433. **Michelle Renee**[12] **Kirby** (Wanda Sue[11] Petty, Joan Dorothy[10] Wilson, Elaine Maxine[9] Webster, Benjamin Harrison[8], William Daniel[7], John H.[6], Samuel[5], Joseph Stancel[4], Samuel[3], Thomas[2], Thomas[1]), born 26 Aug 1976 in Parkersburg, Wood County, West Virginia. She married on 27 Dec 1996 in Parkersburg, Wood County, West Virginia **Matthew James Moore**, born 17 Jan 1975 in Parkersburg, Wood County, West Virginia, son of Hilton James Moore and Linda Lou Wilson.

Children of Michelle Renee Kirby and Matthew James Moore were as follows:
   451   i   **Kylie Page**[13] **Moore**, born 19 Sep 1998 in Vilseck, Germany.
   452   ii   **Cassady Nicole**[13] **Moore**, born 10 Dec 2000 in Lawton, Oklahoma.

INDEX OF NAMES

(--)
  Julia Ann 29
  Rhoda 40
(---)
  Lyn 31
(---)
  Elizabeth 103
(---)
  Elizabeth 114
ALDEN
  John 41, 46
  Sarah 47
ALLEN
  Sandra 116, 131
ANDERSON
  Clarence 94
  Florence Rowena 70, 95
  Francis Ellen (Webster) ... 94
  Mary 115, 130
ARMSTRONG
  Mary Ann 69, 94
AUGUSTINE
  Laura 69, 83
  Reuben [1849-1872] 84
BATCHELDER
  Susannah 9, 18
BERG
  Juia 118
  Julia 106
BERNARDO
  Ann 115

BLACKMER
  Anna 46, 47, 48
BLACKSTONE
  Cassius 81
  Fannie (Webster) 81
BLANCHARD
  Ginny Fern (Webster) ... 122, 147
  Joseph Jules Sr. 123
  Joseph Jules, Sr. 147
  Joseph Jules[11], Jr. .. 147, 161
  Justin Joseph[12] 161
  Maegan Rae[12] 161
  Peggy[11] 148
  Tammy Darlene (Collins) 147, 161
BLAZER
  Sharon Lee (Haefner) 148
  Sharon Lee (HAEFNER) 124
  Stacey Lynne[11] 149
  Steven Lowell 148
BONNETTE
  Ginny Fern (Webster) ... 122, 147
  Robert Joseph 123, 147
BOYER
  Avereil Janis (Hurch) ... 116, 132
  Charles 116, 132
  Richard Edward[11] 132

BRACK
  Barry Gene, Jr. 147
  Stacey Ann (Nash) 147
BRADFORD
  William 46
BREWER
  Sarah 1
BRICKLE
  (---) 112
  Selma (Webster) 112
BRIDGER
  Joane 47
BRIEGHTOL
  Abbie (Webster) 81
  Roy 82
BUCK
  Blanche Bernice 96, 109
BURNHAM
  Elizabeth 8, 15
CAGLE
  Gene 103, 113
  Maxine D. (Webster) 103, 113
  Mickey[10] 113
  Rexter Vernon[10] 113
CARLSON
  Alice Jane (Carlson) 104
  Alice Jane (Webster) 117
  Alice Lorraine[10] 117
  Curtiss Darrell[10] 118
  Darrell 104, 117
CARNER
  Metcalf 112
  Phyllis (Webster) 112
CARR
  Mary 17, 24
  Sarah 17, 28
CARTER

Abraham[5] 19
Elizabeth (Webster) ... 11, 19
Elizabeth[5] 19
Ephraim[5] 19
John 12, 19
John[5] 19
Mary (Webster) 12, 19
Mary[5] 20
Moses[5] 20
Nathaniel[5] 19
Sarah[5] 20
Thomas 12, 19
Thomas W.[5] 19
CHASE
  Abigail (Webster) 23
  Anna (Webster) 23
  Stephen 23
  Trueworthy 23
CLUDAS
  Wilemina Johanna "Minnie"
  .... 84, 99
COLLINS
  Dorothy (Webster) 16, 23
  Jonathan 16, 23
  Samuel[5] 23
  Tammy Darlene 147, 161
COOPER
  Martha 48
CORNELSEN
  Bonnie Lou 120
  Herman David [1903-1952]
  119
COX
  M. Marjorie (Webster) .. 102
  Mamie Mae 96
  Paul 102
CROSS
  John C. 94

166

Minnie Moselle (Webster) 94
CROW
  Fred H. 94
  Laura May (Webster) 94
DAVIS
  Marcy[5] 20
  Miriam (Webster) 12, 20
  Philip 12, 20
  Webster[5] 20
DEARBORN
  Julia Ann 32
DECK
  Susanah 78, 97
DENHAM
  Benjamin 33
DENNEY
  Bernice Elizabeth .. 110, 126
DEPEW
  Polly A. 40, 77
DILLON
  Layrie 108
  Melvia Layrie 123
DOLE
  Arthur 85
  Maggie Malinda (Webster) 85
DREW
  Lucy 23, 31
DUDLEY
  Anna 14, 22
  Phebe (Webster) 14
  Stephen 14
DURIAN
  Emma 95
EASTMAN
  Abigail 18, 30
ELLIOTT
  Bernard 19
EMMONS
  Joseph 3, 5
  Mary 3
ENG
  Ruth 135, 153
FARMER
  Daryl Lee[10] 126
  David Alan[10] 125
  Debra Ann[10] 125
  Deidra Alane[10] 126
  Denise Annette[10] 125
  Donald Lee 108, 125
  Doris Jane (Unruh) 108, 125
FELLOWS
  Joseph[4] 11
  Samual 7
  Samuel 11
  Samuel[4] 11
  Sarah (Webster) 7, 11
FERGUSON
  Kathleen Louise 120, 133
FIFEILD
  John 7
FIFIELD
  Mary (Webster) 7
FITE
  Ruth 104, 117
FLETCHER
  Grace 30
FOWLER
  Elizabeth (Webster) 8
  Josiah 8
FRY
  Charles Sylvester[8] 83
  Frank L.[8] 83
  Harriet (Webster) 69, 82
  Kate O.[8] 83

Mary Jane 83
Virgil 69, 83
FULLENWITER
Waneta 86, 109
FULLER
Deborah 27, 33, 41
Doctor Samuel 41, 42
Dr. Samuel 44
Edward 44
June 102, 112
Robert 44
Simeon 41, 50
Ziba 41
GABLE
Maggie 84, 100
GARRETT
(---) 83
Mary Jane (Fry) 83
GEORGE
Elizabeth 13, 21
Mildred 116, 131
GIDDINGS
Carl 85, 101
Chester[9] 101
Clarice[9] 101
Deborah (Webster) 8
Edna[9] 101
Marion[9] 101
Mary Etta (Webster) 85, 101
Mildred[9] 101
Zebulon 8
GODFREY
Sarah 3, 6
GREELEY
Mary 7, 11
GREEN
Lyman 40, 78
Nancy O. (Webster) ... 40, 78

GRIFFITH
Geraldine 112
GRUVER
(---) 113
Mary (Webster) 113
GWYNN
Francis Joan 121, 134
HACKLER
Herman 86, 109
Nora Mae[9] 109
Ruth Lorena (Webster) ... 86, 109
HAEFNER
Carol Lynne[10] 124
Clarice Elsie (Unruh) 108, 124
Norman Ludwig 108, 124
Sharon Lee[10] 124, 148
Steven Lowell 124
HAHN
Angela Rae 157
HALLOCK
Carolyn 115, 130
HARPER
Frankie 108, 124
HARTLEY
Terri Louise 151
HOCH
Nelva Ruth 108
HOLIDAY
Kathryn 102, 113
HOLLEY
Ann Marie[10] 125
Erma Mae (Unruh) 108, 125
Eugene Quentin[10] 125
Jennie Geneva[10] 125
William C 108, 125
HOPKINS

John Richard 122, 138
Shirley Enola (Knight) . 122, 138
Sophie Cybele[11] 146
HOUSER
Peggy 106, 122
HUCKABEE
(---) 137, 159
Cynthia Loraine (Wilson)
.... 137, 158
HURCH
Amanda Jane[11] 131
Avereil Janis[10] 116, 132
Billie Joy[10] 116
Carolyn (Hallock).. 115, 130
Charles Wesley[10] ... 115, 130
Christopher John[11] 132
Daniel Otis[11] 131
David Lynn[11] 131
Erin Elizabeth[11] 131
George 103, 115
Georgia Dawn[10] 116
Gerald Gene[10] 115, 130
Gilbert Allen[11] 131
Gilbert Leslie[10] 116, 131
Janet (Waldschmidt)..... 116, 132
Judy (Schaaf) 116, 131
June Marie[11] 131
Mary (Anderson)... 115, 130
Mildred (George) .. 116, 131
Monty Wayne[11] 130
Nicole Lynn[11] 132
Robert Douglas[10] ... 116, 131
Sandra (Allen)........ 116, 131
Timothy Allen[10] 116, 132
Wilma Allene (Webster)
.... 103, 115

HURST
Randy............................ 115
Wendy Karleen (Webster)
.... 115
HUTCHINS
Mary 4
JESTER
Elizabeth Amanda (White)
.... 91
John Charles "Jesse" 91
Nancy Jane................ 69, 83
JOHNSON
Greg Brian[10] 118
Marvin 104, 118
Patricia Lillian (Webster)
.... 104, 118
Paul Ryan[10] 118
Teresa Lynn[10] 118
JOHNSTON
N. A. 103, 114
Pauline (Webster).. 103, 113
JONES
Christopher 46
JUDKINS
Hannah........................... 4, 9
KARLEY
Dorothy................. 103, 115
KEEFER
Lillian 85, 103
KELLY
Robert 116
Sandra Sue (Webster).... 116
KING
Edwin R. 103, 114
Edwin[10] 114
Ernest[10] 114
Jill Charlene 127
Norma Geraldine (Webster)

.... 103, 114
KIRBY
   Karl Wayne 136, 157
   Michelle Renee[12] ... 157, 164
   Rebecca Diane[12] 157
   Wanda Sue (Petty). 136, 157
KLASSEN
   Francess Lorraine .. 108, 126
KNAPP
   Angela Renee (Wilson) 138, 160
   Luca Dru 138, 160
   Sydney Renee[12] 160
KNIGHT
   Donald[10] 122
   Gloria[10] 122
   Noel Johnson 106, 122
   Shirley Enola[10] 122, 138
   Virginia Enola (Webster)
   .... 106, 121
LADD
   Abigail (Webster) 14
   Elizabeth 7, 11
   Stephen 14
LANDWEHR
   Anita Marie[11] 134
LANE
   Abigail[3] 6
   Deborah 12, 21
   Elizabeth[3] 6
   John[3] 6
   Joshua[3] 6
   Samuel[3] 6
   Sarah 3
   Sarah[3] 6
   Thomas[3] 6
   William 3, 6
LANGSFORD

(--) 21
(---) 12
LEE
   Bridget 44
   Josephine 44
   Lida 85, 100
LEROY
   Caroline 30
LEWIS
   Abraham 69, 95
   Frank[8] 95
   Nancy (Webster) 69, 95
LINDSEY
   Elihu 40, 78
   Elihu Jr.[7] 79
   Nancy O. (Webster) ... 40, 78
   William[7] 79
LINKE
   Lvonne 108, 123
LIOTTI
   Violet Louise 121, 137
LYSELL
   Denise Ann (Webster) ... 117
   Mark 117
MACE
   James Andrew, Sr .. 136, 157
   James Andrew[12], Jr 157
   Tyler Levi[12] 157
   Wanda Sue (Petty). 136, 157
MAHUGH
   Bart Calvin 151
   Christine Elaine (Mooney)
   151
MAIN
   A. E 83
   Kate O. (Fry) 83
MANUELS
   Almyra May (Webster) ... 84,

99
Edith[9] 100
Pearl[9] 100
William 84, 100
William[9] 100
MARKS
   Angie Lorraine 147, 161
MATTHEWS
   Doris 129
MAYER
   Cacilia 103, 114
MCCARTHY
   Cathleen Myer 138, 160
MCEVERS
   Barbara Elaine (Unruh) 123, 148
   Melanie Shanna[11] 148
   Timothy 124, 148
MERRIMAN
   Donald 116
   Georgia Dawn (Hurch) .. 116
MICK
   Reatric 108, 124
MIESSE
   Christine Erin 151
MILES
   Angelia Dawn[12] 154, 163
   Deborah Sue (Wilson) .. 135, 153
   Laban Marchmont, II 153
   Laban Marchmont[12] 154
   Laban Marchmont[12], III. 163
   Laban Marchmont[13], IV. 164
   Laban Marchmort II 135
   Summer Ann (Trent) 154, 163
MILLER
   (---) 113

Lota (Webster) 113
MITCHELL
   Rhoda 15
MOOMEY
   Jacob 65, 72
   John Jacob 74
   Mary Magdalene 40, 64
MOONEY
   Carol Elaine (Webster). 129, 151
   Christine Elaine[12] 151
   Christine Erin (Miesse).. 151
   Larry Morris 129, 151
   Terri Louise (Hartley) ... 151
   Timothy Andrew[12] 151
   William Lee[12] 151
MOORE
   Cassady Nicole[13] 164
   Kylie Page[13] 164
   Matthew James 157, 164
   Michelle Renee (Kirby) 157, 164
MULLINS
   Alice 48
   Priscilla 41, 47
   William 47
MULLYNS
   John 47
NAHR
   Gretel 103, 114
NASH
   Angie Lorraine (Marks) 147, 161
   Katie Meshail[12] 161
   Leo Quinton, Jr. 147
   Leo Quinton[11], III .. 147, 160
   Pamela Kay (Webster).. 122, 146

Quinton Jr. 122
Stacey Ann[11] 147
NAY
Abigail (Webster) 9
Abigail[3] 9, 10
Ebenezer[3] 9
Hannah[3] 9
John 4, 9
John[3] 9
Joseph[3] 10
Samuel[3] 9
Sarah[3] 9
NEWMAN
Barbara Elaine (Unruh) 123, 148
Keith Andrew[11] 148
Lawrence 124, 148
Wendy Collete[11] 148
NICHOLSON
Lelah Bernice 112, 129
OLDFIELD
Laveta Fern 86, 104
OLLENBERGER
Nora 86, 107
PAGE
Sarah 17, 29
PATLAN
Aaron D.[12] 159
Christopher D.[12] 159
PATTERSON
Jennie Mae 94
PERRSON
Gene 138
Kaitlin[11] 146
Shirley Enola (Knight) .. 138
PERRY
Sarah 32
PERSSON

Gene 122
Shirley Enola (Knight) .. 122
PETERSON
Billie Joy (Hurch) 116
Harold 116
PETTY
Cheryl Ann[11] 136, 158
Joan Dorothy (Wilson) . 121, 135
Judith Lynn[11] 136
Kelly Diane[11] 136
Lucinda Jane[11] 136, 156
Marvin Arno 121, 135
Wanda Sue[11] 136, 157
PLUMMER
Ann 48
POOL
Esther 21
PORTER
Barbara Kay (Webster). 115, 130
Darin[11] 130
Ronald 115, 130
PRIESTAP
Anne Marie 134, 152
QUIMBY
Abigail (Webster) 8
David 8
QUINTON
Melanie 135, 155
RIDER
Inez Ruth (Webster) 106
Noah Eugene 106
RIFFEL
Ruth 106, 123
ROWE
Robert 5
ROYCE

172

Ella Maude (Webster) 85, 104
Harold[9] 104
Marcellas[9] 104
Revillow 85, 104
SAMPSON
Abraham 46, 47
Rebecca 47
SAMSON
Henry 41, 48
James 48
Penelope 48
Rebecca 46, 48
SANDS
Barbara 116, 132
SARGENT
Alice 24, 32
Lydia 17, 23
Mary 5
SAVAGE
Joshua 21
Sally (Webster) 21
SCHAAF
Judy 116, 131
SCOTT
Hannah 64, 81
Ramona Danielle ... 135, 155
SCULL
Cora T. 82
SHAW
Abiah 4
SIMCIC
Josephine Loraine .. 121, 137
SMITH
Berry John 136
Brenda 135, 155
Kelly Diane (Petty) 136
SNIDER

Angela Rae (Hahn) 157
Christa Diane[12] 157
David Robert 136, 156
Jason David[12] 156
Lucinda Jane (Petty) 136, 156
SPARROW
Jacob 78
Laurel (Webster) 78
SPENCER
Brandi Jean 135, 155
SPONGBERG
Margaret 104, 116
SPURRIER
Mabel A. 99, 111
STANCEL
Dorothy 8, 15
STANDISH
Alexander 46, 47
Barbara 45
Captain Myles 41, 45
Lora 46, 47
STANIAN
Mary 8, 12
STUART
Elizabeth 8, 12
STUBBS
(---) 112
Gloria (Webster) 112
STUCKY
Carol Lynne (Haefner) .. 124
Gary Lynn 124
SULLOWAY
Alice (Webster) 12, 20
Benjamin[5] 20
Greeley[5] 20
Jacob 12, 20
Jacob[5] 20

John[5] 20
SWAINE
  Anne[3] 6
  Caleb[3] 5
  John[3] 5
  Mary 3
  Mary[3] 5
  Mehitable[3] 5
  Sarah[3] 6
  William 3, 5
  William[3] 5
SWALLANDER
  Alban 86, 108
  Delores Lamar[9] 108
  Minnie Alvina (Webster) 86, 108
Teatsworth
  Ann Elizabeth 40
TEATSWORTH
  Ann Elizabeth 76
THOMAS
  Amgelia Dawn (Miles) .. 163
  Angelia Dawn (Miles) ... 154
  Emma 63
  John Ellis 154, 163
  Tanaya Cheyene[13] 163
THOMERSON
  Glenn 127
  Julia Christene (Webster) 127
TONGUE
  Martha 5
TRASK
  Barbara (Webster) 77
  Francis 77
TRENT
  Summer Ann 154, 163
TUPPER

John R. 82
Mary E. (Webster) 82
ULLOM
  Brandon James[12] 158
  Cheryl Ann (Petty) 158
  Christopher Daniel[12] 158
  James Raymond 158
  Nathanial Ryan[12] 158
ULLUM
  Cheryl Ann (Petty) 136
  James Raymond 136
UNRUH
  Barbara Elaine[10] 123, 148
  Bertha Jane (Webster) 86, 107
  Brian J.[10] 126
  Clarice Elsie[9] 108, 124
  Doris Jane[9] 108, 125
  Elman J.[9] 107, 123
  Erma Mae[9] 108, 125
  Francess Lorraine (Klassen) 108, 126
  Frankie (Harper) 108, 124
  Harold Marvin[9] 108
  John F. 86, 107
  Jonas Boyd[9] 108, 126
  Louis Daniel[9] 108, 124
  Lvonne (Linke) 108, 123
  Milvia Layrie (Dillon) ... 123
  Nelva Ruth (Hoch) 108
  Reatric (Mick) 108, 124
  Steve Louis[10] 124
  Virginia Lee[10] 124
WALDRON
  Abigail 8, 13
WALDSCHMIDT
  Janet 116, 132
WATSON

Inez Ruth (Webster) 106
Ralph 106
WATTS
Mary 14
WEBB
Alice Lorraine (Carlson) 117
Howard 118
WEBSTER
(--) (Langsford) 21
(---) (Langsford) 12
Abbie Ann[7] 63
Abbie[8] 81
Abiah 4
Abigail (Eastman) 18, 30
Abigail (Waldron) 8, 13
Abigail[2] 4, 9
Abigail[3] 8
Abigail[4] 14
Abigail[5] 23
Abigail[6] 32
Adelaide M.[6] 61
Alice (Sargent) 24, 32
Alice Jane[9] 104, 117
Alice[3] 7
Alice[4] 12, 20
Almyra May[8] 84, 99
Alvoretta[7] 78
Amina[7] 78
Ann (Bernardo) 115
Ann Elizabeth (Teatsworth
.... 76
Ann Elizabeth (Teatsworth)
.... 40
Anna (Dudley) 14, 22
Anna[4] 12
Anna[5] 23
Anne Marie (Priestap) .. 134, 152

Arthur H.[8] 96, 109
Arthur[9] 100
Auristella[6] 32
Baker Junior[7] 81
Baker[6] 31, 63
Baker[7] Junior 63
Barbara (Sands) 116, 132
Barbara Kay[10] 115, 130
Barbara[7] 77
Benjamin Harrison[8] . 85, 104
Benjamin[3] 7, 12
Benjamin[4] 12, 14, 17, 29
Benjamin[5] 21, 29
Benjamin[6] 31
Benjamin[7] 64
Bernice Elizabeth (Denney)
.... 126
Bernice Elizabeth (Denney_
.... 110
Bertha Jane[8] 86, 107
Bety[5] 28
Billy[10] 113
Blanche Bernice (Buck) . 96, 109
Bob Rex Alvin[9] 106, 123
Bobby[10] 123
Burnham[4] 17
Burnham[5] 24, 32
Cacilia (Mayer) 103, 114
Captain Ebenezer[4] 18, 29
Carol Elaine[11] 129, 151
Caroline (LeRoy) 30
Caroline Adelia[7] 63
Charles Eugene[8] 84
Charles G.[8] 82
Charles Sylvester[8] 94
Clayton Emery[8] 94
Cora T. (Scull) 82

175

Dale Douglas[10] 120, 133
Daniel Clay[8] 85, 103
Daniel Keith[10] 117
Daniel W.[7] 77
David Denney[10] 127
David F.[6] 33
David[4] 16, 17, 28
David[5] 27
David[6] 40, 75
Davison[5] 22, 31
Davison[6] 31
Davison[7] 63
Deacon Samuel[3] 8, 15
Deborah (Fuller) 27, 33
Deborah (Lane) 12, 21
Deborah[3] 8
Denise Ann[10] 117
Doris Matthews 129
Dorothy (Karley) ... 103, 115
Dorothy (Stancel) 8, 15
Dorothy[4] 13, 16, 23
Dorothy[9] 102
Douglas Clifford[11] . 134, 152
Earl[9] 107
Ebenezer[2] 3, 9
Ebenezer[3] 9, 18
Edward Daniel[10] 114
Elaine Maxine[9] 106, 121
Electra Ann[8] 85
Eliza Hannah (Yoakam) . 69, 82
Eliza[5] 29
Elizabeth "Bessy" (Wining) 85, 102
Elizabeth (---) 103, 114
Elizabeth (Burnham) ... 8, 15
Elizabeth (Carter) 19
Elizabeth (George) 13, 21
Elizabeth (LADD) 7, 11
Elizabeth (Stuart) 8, 12
Elizabeth[3] 8
Elizabeth[4] 11, 13, 17, 19
Elizabeth[6] 31
Ella Maude[8] 85, 104
Elmer Earl[8] 96
Emerson[9] 107
Emma (Durian) 95
Emma (Thomas) 63
Emma Josephine[7] 70
Enos[10] 112
Esther (Pool) 21
Ethel May[8] 96
Evelyn Marie (Zohlen) . 134, 152
Evelyn[9] 107
Everett Winston[9] ... 103, 114
Fannie[8] 81
Florence Rowena (Anderson) 70, 95
Florence[8] 84
Forrest[10] 112
Francis Ellen[8] 94
Francis Mariah[7] 64
Francis[5] 28, 61
Frehling Sylvester[7] 69, 95
Gary Dean[10] 117
George[8] 97
Gerald[9] 102, 112
Geraldine (Griffith) 112
Geraldine Marilyn[10] 112
Gertrude[9] 100
Ginny Fern[10] 122, 147
Gloria[10] 112
Grace (Fletcher) 30
Gretel (Nahr) 103, 114
Hannah (Judkins) 4, 9

Hannah (Scott) 64, 81
Hannah[2] 3
Hannah[7] 63
Harriet[7] 69, 82
Henry[5] 29
Honorable Daniel 3
Horatio[6] 61
Howard Emerson[9] . 110, 126
Howard Lincoln[8] 85, 102
Howard[9] 99
Ian Havre[12] 152
Inez Ruth[9] 106
Ira[8] 97
Isaac[2] 4
Jacob[4] 13, 21
Jacob[5] 29
Jacob[7] 69
James[10] 112
Jennie Mae (Patterson) 94
Jennie Orilla[8] 94
Jerry Lee[10] 117
Jill Charlene (King) 127
John Charles[7] 70
John David[7] 78, 97
John Ellsworth[8] 84, 100
John H.[6] 40, 64
John Raymond[9] 100
John[2] 4
John[4] 14
John[5] 22, 28
John[6] 32
John[7] 64
Joseph Norman[8] 82
Joseph Stancel[4] 17, 24
Joseph[4] 14
Joseph[5] 27
Joseph[6] 40
Josephine Maude[8] 95

Joshua[2] 4
Joshua[3] 8, 13
Joshua[4] 14
Joshua[5] 21
Julia (Berg) 106, 118
Julia Ann (--) 29
Julia Ann (Dearborn) 32
Julia Christene[10] 127
June (Fuller) 102, 112
Katherine Ann[10] 133
Kathleen Louise (Ferguson)
 .... 120, 133
Kathrine Ann[10] 117
Kathryn (Holiday) . 102, 113
Kenneth[9] 101
Larry Joe[10] 120, 134
Larry Wayne[10] 116, 132
Larry[10] 112
Laura (Augustine) 69, 83
Laura May[8] 94
Laurel[7] 78
Laurence[8] 82
Laverne[9] 101
Laveta Fern (Oldfield) 86, 104
Lawrence Lester[8] 86, 107
Layrie (Dillon) 108
Leander[6] 32
Lee McKinley[8] 86
Lee McKinley[9] 109
Lelah Bernice (Nicholson)
 .... 112, 129
Lester[9] 107
Lida (Lee) 85, 100
Lillian (Keefer) 85, 103
Lois[6] 31
Loraine Eleanor[10] 111
Lota[10] 113

Louisana (---) 63
Lucille[9] 102
Lucy (Drew).............. 23, 31
Lucy[5] 22
Lucy[6] 32
Lydia (Sargent) 17, 23
Lydia[5] 28
Lyn (---)........................... 31
M. Lafayette[7] 69, 94
M. Marjorie[9]................. 102
Mabel A. (Spurrier). 99, 111
Madlyn E.[9] 102
Maggie (Gable) 84, 100
Maggie Malinda[8] 85
Malinda[7].......................... 69
Mamie Mae (Cox)............ 96
Manly[6] 40
Margaret (Spongberg) .. 104, 116
Marion Jonas[8].......... 85, 100
Marrium[9]...................... 100
Martha[4] 12
Martha[5] 29
Mary 5
Mary (Carr)..................... 24
Mary (Greeley)............. 7, 11
Mary (Hutchins)................ 4
Mary (Stanian) 8, 12
Mary (Watts).................. 14
Mary Ann (Armstrong)... 69, 94
Mary Carr 17
Mary E.[8] 82
Mary Etta[8] 85, 101
Mary Jane[6] 40
Mary K. (Yost)................ 82
Mary Magdalene (Moomey)
.... 40, 64

Mary Magdaline (Moomey)
....................................72
Mary[10] 113
Mary[2] 3
Mary[3] 7
Mary[4] 12, 13, 19
Mary[7] 78
Maxine D.[9] 103, 113
Milton[9]......................... 101
Minerva[6] 32
Minnie Alvina[8] 86, 108
Minnie Moselle[8].............. 94
Miriam[4]..................... 12, 20
Nancy (Whitcomb).......... 61
Nancy Jane (Jester)... 69, 83, 91
Nancy O.[6] 40, 78
Nancy Whitcomb 28
Nancy[5] 22
Nancy[7] 69, 95
Nanny[4] 17
Nathaniel[5] 29
Nellie[8] 81
Nora (Ollenberger) .. 86, 107
Norma Geraldine[9].. 103, 114
Pamela Kay[10] 122, 146
Patricia Lillian[9] 104, 118
Patty[6]................................ 32
Pauline[9]................. 103, 113
Pearl H. (Whittenberg) ... 85, 101
Peggy (Houser) 106, 122
Phebe[4]..............................14
Phyllis[10] 112
Polly A. (DePew) 40, 77
Polly[5] 22, 28
Rachel[4]............................ 17
Randall Harry[9] 106, 122

178

Reginald Dale[9] 105, 118
Rhoda (--) 40
Rhoda (---) 77
Rhoda (Mitchell) 15
Richard Eugene[11] 129
Richard[7] 78
Robert 109
Robert Stanton[10] 114
Ronald Daniel[9] 104, 117
Ruth (Fite) 104, 117
Ruth (Riffel) 106, 123
Ruth Lorena[8] 86
Ruth Lorena[9] 109
Ruth[5] 28
Sally[5] 21
Samuel[4] 13, 16, 17
Samuel[5] 23, 24, 27, 33
Samuel[7] 78
Sandra Sue[10] 116
Sarah 1
Sarah (--) 4
Sarah (Carr) 17, 28
Sarah (Godfrey) 3
Sarah (Page) 17
Sarah (Perry) 32
Sarah E.[7] 78
Sarah Page 29
Sarah[2] 3, 6
Sarah[3] 7, 11
Sarah[4] 12, 13, 16, 17
Sarah[5] 21, 22, 27
Selma[10] 112
Senator Daniel[5] 30
Simeon M.[7] 69, 82
Simeon[6] 40, 77
Stanley Ross[9] 99, 111
Stanton Frank[10] 111
Starlin S.[6] 33

Susanah (Deck) 97
Susanha (Deck) 78
Susannah (Batchelder). 9, 18
Susannah[5] 22
Tayte Margaux[12] 152
Thomas 1
Thomas Carr[5] 29
Thomas[1] 1
Thomas[10] 113
Thomas[2] Jr. 3, 6
Thomas[3] 7, 11
Thomas[4] 12, 16, 21
Thomas[5] 22, 29
Tonya Maria[11] 133
Velma[9] 107
Violet[9] 101
Virgil Franklin[8] 85, 101
Virginia Enola[9] 106, 121
Waldron 22
Waldron[4] 14
Waldron[5] Junior 22
Waneta (Fullenwiter) 86, 109
Warren Frances[9] 103, 116
Wendell Sherwood[9] 103, 115
Wendy Karleen[10] 115
Wesley Blaine[8] 95
Wilemina Johanna "Minnie"
  (Cludas) 84, 99
William Daniel[7] 69, 83
William Eugene[10] .. 112, 129
William Wesley[8] 84, 99
William Wining[9] ... 102, 113
William[4] 13, 14
William[5] 22
William[9] 109
Wilma Allene[9] 103, 115
WELLBORN
Katherine Ann (Webster)

.... 133
Kathrine Ann (Webster) 117
Kathryn Jennifer[11] 133
William 117, 133
WHITCOMB
  Nancy 28, 61
WHITE
  Elizabeth Amanda 91
WHITTENBERG
  Pearl H. 85, 101
WILLIAMS
  Edward 5
WILSON
  Angela Renee[11] 138, 160
  Anthony Michael[11] 138, 159
  Beth Ann[11] 135
  Brandi Jean (Spencer) .. 135, 155
  Brenda (Smith) 135, 155
  Cathleen Myer (McCarthy)
    .... 138, 160
  Cynthia Loraine[11] .. 137, 158
  David Patrick[11] 135, 154
  Deborah Sue[11] 135, 153
  Derek Ryan[12] 156
  Diana L.[12] 159
  Dore Verl 106, 121
  Dylan Michael[12] 160
  Elaine Maxine (Webster)
    .... 106, 121
  Francis Joan (Gwynn) .. 121, 134
  Haylee Elizabeth[12] 155
  Joan Dorothy[10] 121, 135
  Josephine Loraine (Simcic)
    .... 121, 137
  Joshua Michael[12] 153
  Kamree Danielle[12] 156

Koty Ditto[12] 154
Melanie (Quinton). 135, 155
Michael James[10] 121, 137
Michael Joseph Verl[12] ... 159
Michele Lynette[11] .. 137, 159
Michelle Nicole[12] 153
Patrick Spencer[12] 156
Phillip Timothy[11] Sr. 135
Phillip Timothy[11], Sr, ... 155
Phillip Timothy[12], Jr. 156
Ramona Danielle (Scott)
  .... 135, 155
Rodney Dale[10] 121, 134
Ruby Elaine (Winkler) . 135, 154
Ruth (Eng) 135, 153
Shawn Joseph[11] 135
Shawn Joseph[11], Sr 154
Shawn Joseph[12], Jr. 154
Steven Michael[11] ... 134, 153
Steven Ross[10] 121, 137
Tiffani Gwynn[12] 154
Tyler Christian[12] 156
Violet Louise (Liotti).... 121, 137
WINING
  Elizabeth "Bessy" 85, 102
WINKLER
  Ruby Elaine 135, 154
WINSTEAD
  (---) 137, 159
  Michele Lynette (Wilson)
    .... 137, 159
WONDERS
  Joseph 81
  Nellie (Webster) 81
YOAKAM
  Eliza Hannah 69, 82

YODER
  Daniel E. 96
  Elmer E. 95
  Ethel May (Webster) 96
  Josephine Maude (Webster)
  95
YOST
  Mary K. 82
ZOHLEN
  Evelyn Marie 134, 152

About the Author

Dale Douglas Webster is the son of Reginald and Julia (Berg) Webster. He was born on February 5, 1945 in Wichita, Kansas. Dale graduated from Wichita State University in 1967 with a Bachelor of Arts degree in mathematics, from Oklahoma University in 1968 with a Certificate in meteorology, and from the University of Oregon in 1976 with a Master of Business Administration degree.

He served over twenty years within the U.S. and overseas as an Air Force officer in meteorology, transportation, and computer science. After retiring from the U.S. Air Force in 1987, Dale worked in the Washington, D.C. metropolitan area as a computer software consultant. He retired completely in 2003 and relocated to Austin, Texas to be with his grandchildren.

Dale has been married to Kathleen Ferguson for forty-two years. They have one son, Douglas. Doug and his wife, Anne, have two sons, Cole and Ian, and a daughter, Tayte.

He has been researching his family history for twenty years. He is a member of the Mayflower Society, the Alden Kindred, and the Sons of the American Revolution. If you have any information that can update or expand this work, please contact:

Dale D. Webster
10720 Bay Laurel Trail
Austin, Texas 78750
(512) 918-0732
Thewebsters2@earthlink.net

www.ingramcontent.com/pod-product-compliance
Lightning Source LLC
Chambersburg PA
CBHW072129160426
43197CB00012B/2038